# AUTUMN AND SPRING ANNALS

Quentin S. Crisp was born in 1972, in North Devon, U.K. He studied Japanese at Durham University and graduated in 2000. He has had fiction published by Tartarus Press, PS Publishing, Eibonvale Press and others.

QUENTIN S. CRISP

# AUTUMN AND SPRING ANNALS

THIS IS A SNUGGLY BOOK

Copyright © 2022 by Quentin S. Crisp.
All rights reserved.


ISBN: 978-1-64525-117-0

## Contents

November / 11
December / 55
January / 97
February / 141
March / 181
April / 229

# AUTUMN AND SPRING ANNALS

# NOVEMBER
*(2017)*

## 1ˢᵗ November (Wednesday)

The lid won't open
On the kettle anymore.
Brokenness outstrips
My capacity to fix.
How long will this go on for?


I rely on lives
That need fixing in their turn—
Mutual deficit.
Even the relationships
That would fix are now breaking.


Obituary—
As if something's completed.
For someone, perhaps.
For the others, unresolved
Stresses become visible.

On the graves, squirrels
Scamper. Living heraldry
Of nature, passed by.
To be so deep in the past
That you are not anywhere.


Evil all around.
Not evil people, as such,
But agents blandly
Introducing evil where
None was before. Just normal.


So they grant rights to
A robot but not women.
Why are you so shocked?
This is the very future
That you're fighting for, writ small.


Now faces can be
Randomly generated
Any photograph
I see could be a fake. Thus
Turing degraded us all.

## 2nd November (Thursday)

*In media res.*
Not only the beginning
But the end, always.
Still, a lifetime, like mine, frames,
Among these things, its own doom.


Dying. My wretched
Gains all spilt away like books
From collapsing shelves.
All I installed in place of
Dreams reverting now to dreams.


Sheer numbers convict
Me of madness, perhaps. How
Can I disagree?
Yet how can I be other
Than this self-focusing me?


Water from the tap—
So cold now my fingers ache.
Such things make me think
Of Pete. This is what he's left:
Occasions to be, to talk.

### 3rd November (Friday)

"Stop watching the news."
Should I make this my praxis?
It's true: fear sells.
While I'm thus hypnotised, what
Passes is this only life.


Ever attentive,
Pre-empting offence I might
Give without knowing;
Such expectation becomes
A vexation, and so on.


### 4th November (Saturday)

Sleepless, searching for
A pen, I think of the things
You've left in my room.
We will not resume the days
From which they were pieces played.

"I have constructed
A machine to dream my dreams
Instead of me, so
I can sleep in vacant night."
Yes, quite amazing—but why?


Skating on hailstones
In the dark morning, dragged by
A thunder-spurred dog.
How wonderful that I was
Sunk so deep in my own life.


I can't adjust to
The way people seem to start
A conversation
By text, then drop into long
Silence, no "over and out".


On the ground, mixed leaves,
A softening festival
Beyond all census.
But here where they're brown on brown,
All one shape, deep, bury me.

## 5th November (Sunday)

Malapropism
And malodorousness: linked
Infelicities.
My logos, not gnosis, in
Effect is halitosis.


Friends die; on I age,
Wounded and wounding, and on.
Life just is suspense.
Even if there's no answer,
The question, at least, makes sense.


Pacific islands
Are threatened by rising seas.
We're in denial,
Say those who, themselves, won't face
The role technology plays.


Almost five o'clock.
A firework's climbing burn
Culminates in crows.
Shaken from the crowns of trees,
Cawing their old, bone-tongued peal.

## 6th November (Monday)

My heart is cratered
With a landscape no one seems
To recognise. Love
Does not thrive here, yet in its
Nameless way it is alive.


Destiny? Perhaps.
Like a river's eroded
Course, this solitude.
And like a river, I can't
Turn back to correct that crook.


I'm responsible
For what I can't control? I
Don't think so. Well then,
Let the future roll and roll;
It's ditched my helpless freedom.

Last night the usual
Dull artillery, echoed
Each year by habit.
How subdued the fireworks feel,
Like the fortune I have lived.


How sweet not to care.
(It will not last. It will not
Last.) How needful to
My soul that I should care. (It
Will not last. It will not last.)


My calendar shows,
For November, a dusky
View of Ladram Bay.
I've inked dates in, a tactic
To meet this year-end pressure.


Even when I'm dead
It won't be understood that
I've already said
That you'll be reading this when
I'm dead, not understanding.

## 7<sup>th</sup> November (Tuesday)

We are told we are
Not attractive unless we
Are happy alone.
"Fine. I'm happy alone. I
Don't want to be attractive."


Negative. Lucky
In what I have avoided,
Not what I have done.
Behind my eyes, a vision
Of soaring pines, mountain dusk.


The world, where all we
Do takes place; we, the people,
Who all leave the world.
So, all we do here is lay
Flowers at a wayside shrine.


Days have come when it's
Hard to heat this flat. I brush
My hair with the brush
You bought in Kyôto. Twined in
Its tines, my brown and silver.

Does it not affirm
Life to receive an old friend
Who has travelled far?
Is it not pleasing to be
Praised by him for one's bookshelves?


Time to pause, as if
I was dead, as if a test
Was over and I
Knew my score, and all that lay
Ahead was one, last unknown.


## 8<sup>th</sup> November (Wednesday)


Last words. I used to
Think about such things, but now
I don't so much care.
Let death reveal or veil what
It must, and write in my dust.


Tender as embers
In the cold of November,
A presentiment
Of the end, warming me by
What I care to remember.

"What does it feel like?"
"A new tooth coming through, but
I'm too old for that."
Examination. X-rays.
"Wisdom tooth." Should I have known?


The peculiar
Tunnel between Waterloo
And Waterloo East—
Will it someday seem to me,
Like a longed-for home, besouled?


### 9<sup>th</sup> November (Thursday)


Sainsbury's loose carrots.
Always someone bending to
Choose the least blemished.
Wryly I stare at this arse,
For God and humanity.

Jackson Pollock—John
Said—in the full flush of fame,
Cried to his wife: "What
Do they want from me? Can't they
See I've done it?" They can't see.


Like Sydney Carton:
Serious enough to see
What a joke I am.
Friends, what weapons do we have
Who fight for humanity?


Should a quietist,
What's more, unschooled, late-starting,
Join battle? Or is
Victory to ignore this
Noisy war of ignorance?


Bring me my bow of
Hesitation, bring me my
Arrows of decline!
And on my shield, come, let blows
Fall, of Churchlands Pat and Paul!

## 10th November (Friday)


If there's nothing but
The brain, I find no reason
Left to prevent me
Becoming a terrorist
For Puff the Magic Dragon.


Ghostly and brittle,
The slithering clink of glass
From recycling bins.
How specific this world is;
How elusive consciousness.


Strange how meanings twist.
Popularly, a skeptic
Doesn't believe in
Ghosts; in philosophy, he
Doesn't believe in the world.


I can't help thinking
Of Pete's bookshelves. The spines seemed
To imply his hand.
The world is just another
Such collection, but for whom?

Who can I read who
Will not at some point disgust
Me by being wrong?
And what can I ever be,
Then, for others, but other?


### 11<sup>th</sup> November (Saturday)

I never took to
This world—a failed graft. And yet
I never escaped.
Attached by fascination
To its haunt, an earthbound ghost.


I envy humans.
Even those for whom death is
Unacceptable
Choose life. Death plus sex, for them,
Makes yes. Fools. Not for this ghost.


Cloudy November.
I woke well past eleven.

To-do never done.
I am the only dog I
Have in this hopeless, dull fight.


Mist. Rumbles and booms.
Are there still fireworks? Is it
Just trains? I tread through
Wet leaves. Why are we drawn to
The ebbing soul's candle glow?


### 12<sup>th</sup> November (Sunday)

Judgement—division.
But wit is an addition,
Multiplying links.
Tripping, I forget, this world
Never gets wit's mirror-web.


A clear idea
Means a little idea,
Says Burke. Quine dissents,
Invents a pesticide to
Quell possible entities.

Dark now. Electric
Light inside. A teaspoon on
The plastic breadboard.
One of those pensive tingles:
Even if I fail, I live.


For Quine, deserts are
Lovely. But what does 'lovely'
Mean? Let this pot plant
Stand as all there is. Bounded,
It's an endless fount of not.


Why do I fear that
Truth can kill? Who are they that
Speak with such intent?
Since my earliest days, this
Is the world I've been against.


### 13<sup>th</sup> November (Monday)


Sometimes I hear my
Heart beating in my ear and
I'm afraid that when
It stops I'll be deaf. Last night
I lay awake, listening.

Long coach journeys to
Swindon. Anticipation
Of the songs we'd make.
It's all another life. I
Doubt even God remembers.


Not only do I
Go back to nothing; the whole
Journey itself is
Nothing. Nothing with all of
Everything's punishing weight.


Is redness a thing?
How can we speak of red things
Truly if it's not?
Lives lost in this war. What are
These divisive niceties?


You don't understand
How it is. My will is in
Decline just as my
Spirit starts the haggard climb.
Each step—the drag! The fatigue!

Another stagger
As a mace splits my shield with
A shuddering blow.
My fibula's protruding
Through my skin, but on I go.


### 14th November (Tuesday)


Quine's desert is of
Shifting sands. It is X and
Always X, but we
Do not know what X is. See
The veil blown from the dune's ridge.


To study being.
To argue that this fist is
Or is not a thing.
What unseen snake can I grasp
With this logic? Everything.


To be remembered
By those who are forgotten.
To be remembered

By those who are remembered
By those who are forgotten.


Why should I regret
If I had to leave the world
Today? It is done.
Always, what we start from, or
Accomplish, this: It is done.


What do I want but
Play? Being or illusion,
I want to get my
Hands on those variables,
To understand, rearrange.


### 15<sup>th</sup> November (Wednesday)


The accoutrements
Of my vow, in a clutter
Of fascination.
Books and such. Alone, coping,
I go through my devotions.

Yes, it's cold here, but
Is that why we wear clothes? Is
It not a romance
Of tender complicity,
A charmed masque of what's unsaid?


*The Prince of Homburg*
By von Kleist. Someone mentioned
It the other night.
Who was it? Time, place, face come
Clear. The workings of my mind.


We who have taken
A vow of poverty, one
Sinful side-effect
Cannot avoid (God grant us,
Please): the loveliness of books.


Rising I find hard,
But I must concede: morning
Is day's sweetest part.
Ablutions; lone, self-contained
Routine; whitening windows.

About half past three,
The sounds of children going
Home from school. Always,
Some tired child in me responds.
How soon day begins to end.


What ability
Is mine? I am not wise or
Skilled. I have a gift.
An inkwell echoing with
Ghostly sighs. It never dries.


Expanding London.
It takes time to get somewhere.
Such distances, such
Crowds. Two friends find months, then years
Go by between each meeting.


### 16<sup>th</sup> November (Thursday)


To begin this task
Is to die in the shallows,
Having left the shore.
Each time I find the bottom,
It shelves away, deeper, more.

I have begun. That
I can say. I have opened
That ocean door. See!
Devil fish and sea angels.
I must drown or grow strange gills.


So tired. I am judged.
And if I defend myself,
I protest too much.
I tried, and you judged me. Why
Did you judge me? Who are you?


Tudor beams above
An estate agent. Real? Fake?
A billboard (whisky)
Shows a star-reflecting lake.
Haunted by the wild we've slain.


### 17th November (Friday)


Lovecraft made it clear
That he wrote of the defeat

Of nature's fixed laws.
If all is clockwork physics,
Life's true realm is fantasy.


Last night, one a.m.,
Smoking and listening to
*A Crow Looked at Me*,
Thinking how far beyond help
The situation now is.


Wednesday, after dark.
I stopped on the path, listened
To the hidden crows.
I hope they're plotting to draw
The eerie frontiers back in.


The old, dark house where
We were confined with decay
And religious fear,
We've escaped. Into a net,
Dissecting us with bright pins.

## 18ᵗʰ November (Saturday)

Very little now
Seems to give me energy.
Most things just drain it.
I'm vaulting ranks of tombstones
To reach my own grave, and rest.


Gorman uniting
The nation: "Some things we all
Agree on, like blokes
Who hold their money *like this*
At the bar are dicks." Like me.


Change might be worse than
Death, if it means a thing is
Now what it was not.
Thus 'was' receives no rest, but
Is not kept, and 'is' is doomed.


Identity of
Person might be like that of
Nation: porous, but
Real. I am a nation. Some
Deplore even such borders.

Take a film such as
*The Void*. How viscerally
It confronts our age.
Strange operations take us
Beyond. Do we survive this?


Conservative, you
Impute. But no, it's just this:
Love is a sword, forged
In sex and death, that cuts us
Into individuals.


Not to overstate,
But those two years or so were,
Yes, my happiest.
Like a living, seeing eye,
That tenderness. I bless it.


What matters, Parfit
Says, in survival, is not
Identity. In
Hospital, asked, "Who is this?"
He knew: "The love of my life."

### 19th November (Sunday)

Since each object is
A bloom of infinity,
I have fluttered lost.
Better that than branching tags
That flat-pack into science.


These headaches—perhaps
Not just tiredness, or the glow
Of the computer.
The dentist said I clench my
Jaw. Yes, and let others talk.


### 20th November (Monday)

An envelope whose
Style I recognise. Inside,
A cheque: royalties.
Twenty pounds. That decides it:
I'll see New Model Army.

What is this life, then,
But to sail away into
Sadness? With what hope
Do people still have children
Now we're not just surviving?


Envy has defined
My history. I made bad
Choices; I made good.
Now look where we are. The fools
Have won. I envy no one.


For now I still walk
Straight. Grow old into the new,
Ever forwards, sharp,
Cutting like a prow. Sadness
Parts like waves, can't be retraced.


I promise to meet
You next week. It comes. Are we
Still the same people?
Is it a ghost if it's me?
Then I promise to haunt you.

## 21ˢᵗ November (Tuesday)


My obligation
To the dead has been blocked. How
Cruel to allow me
No hearing or verdict, just
Evasion and suspicion.


Funny how I knew
I wasn't meant for work. "Who
Is?" some would counter.
They'd call me degenerate.
God knows, I had to be me.


After long détente
All of our vendettas are
Resurfacing. You
Berate me for not taking
A position. Take this blade.


The sun's last light, or
The city's glow trapped by clouds.
So angry and tired.
You cook up new ways for things
To go wrong. You don't need me.

Lost, contemplating
These theories. When I try to
Apply them I find
There's only one you. For whom
Do we deny our being?


The wind, cold, almost
Tender as a hairdresser's
Fingers. I'm thinning.
And soon I'll shrink entirely
Away. Lies will fill this space.


## 22$^{nd}$ November (Wednesday)


If there is no sum
Greater than the parts, then there
Are only several
Billion lostnesses, like
Mine, terminating in death.


What kind of mind is
This John Rawls to punish his
Readers with vagueness?
A cement mixer presents
One thousand views of cement.

"Not just surviving,"
I wrote, but soon enough we
Might not even be
Surviving. Will this bring back
What we have lost of meaning?


Are morality
And truth two separate things? Then,
How choose between them?
The latter's a losing bet
If not part of the former.


If the end renders
All things meaningless, why try
To confront it with
Meaning? To confront the end,
Then, just is an act of faith.


A sickle moon, low
Above rooftops. In branches
Tilts death's Madonna.
You are the mother. To our
Children, I leave everything.

## 23ʳᵈ November (Thursday)

Last night, sleepless, I
Heard a most uncanny wind.
Quick-slow moans. Something
Shook its shroud. Hovered. Would its
Wings enclose me? It moved on.


I read something by
A just departed friend. It
Ended with a smile.
To disappear and leave just
This riddling smile. What now, John?


I've known an expert
Or two. Undervalued, but
It's still true: they have
Very strange views. Politics
Divide. Meanwhile, who am I?


What comes to mind? For
The ancients, Greek and Chinese:
Always white horses.
Horseness and whiteness abound.
For the moderns: chairs. This desk.

For some I'm the past.
I'm nobody's future. But
For me I'm always
The present. I just have to
Learn to be a better ghost.

### 24th November (Friday)

All these pricks who think
We're living in the Matrix—
Nothing but Earthlings.
They only seem to grasp doubt
Of this world through this-world tech.


I don't know why I
Continue to defer to
Those who do as they
Please. Is anyone playing
The game, or is it just me?


Life is good for some.
That's how it should be. But why

Nor for us? For me?
The time to ask such questions
Was before we could ask them.


"I'll wear a blindfold
To judge the case," says Rawls. "See!
Even blindfolded
I agree with me!" Self-doubt—
Something other people lack.


Questions—those we most
Want answered are larger than
A single lifetime.
Tonight a bomb could end this
Person, survived by questions.


### 25<sup>th</sup> November (Saturday)

First, I assumed I
Was mad. Then a way opened:
Perhaps I was more
Rational than most. Testing,
I'm drawn back to my first thought.

Non-fungible, my
Mind cannot be exchanged for
The rational truth.
There's a remainder, keeping
Me solitary, deranged.


I see things. Their A
And their B are not as mine.
Their deductions seem
To me cross-grained reductions.
Mine seem to them Double Dutch.


Again I have failed.
This time to climb the ladder
Of reason to God.
I'm left with broken reason's
Stilts, a hunchbacked, roving freak.


My younger friends don't
Understand my exhaustion.
My older friends don't
Understand my ambition.
No one adds up the whole sum.

In short, I know death
Is near for me—not quite in
Fear, but short of breath.
And I need air to tell one
Last discriminating thing.


### 26th November (Sunday)


As if this life were
Echo-flames playing out in
Some dying brain. Yet
In this helpless nightmare there
Are quivers of hope, of love.


Varg found that darkness
Was his light. There's no future
In this hate, you say.
I say, if there's a future
Then it must incorporate.


End conflict; preserve
The wild. Optimism is
Necessity; we
Must face dread facts. Meanwhile, we
Slump in the armchair called now.

What's wrong with London
Tonight? This sudden cold and
No Lewisham trains.
And this man—Pally? Psycho?
Worse: both?—repeats, "Just joking."


### 27th November (Monday)

A lone policeman
Winds a cordon round a closed
Police station. From
A passing bus, someone jeers.
Law's a recorded message.


The relief each time
I see a friend who isn't
Dead can't be expressed.
By definition, in fact.
The thread for now unsevered.


Immersed in The Search
For Truth. I mean the twelve-inch
From Thomas Dolby—

A re-mix of 'Dissidents'.
The pleasures of time and space.


Passing offices,
Trees a mesh of silhouette
Against lit windows.
On the train, I lay down my
Print-out. This quiet freedom.


### 28th November (Tuesday)


Gower Street, approached
From a different direction.
The surprise, this late,
Of a bright window full of
Books. But I've no time tonight.


Sitting on a bench
In the dark, in Russell Square,
Eating sandwiches.
This might be the high-tide line
For all future happiness.

It doesn't take much
To incur someone's hatred:
Just an opinion
On gay marriage, or genre,
Or whether we should all die.


The imperative
To be authentic comes with
A strange, implied threat.
Who will punish me if I
Don't care about my life? How?


I'm told no one reads
Books in heaven, despite what
Borges hoped. Why would
They? Then I'll put off dying,
Linger between worlds, and dream.


### 29<sup>th</sup> November (Wednesday)


Losing and winning—
I'm experienced in one,
Therefore I'm biased.
Purge the unproductive? I
Must demur. You see, that's me.

In the fairy tale
I am the beast. Since childhood
I've ached with the thought
Of what waited in me to
Be released. It never was.


David Benatar
Attacked online: "These liberals
Just defeat themselves.
No job. No kids." The net sum
Of my life: lamentation.


Strange how things conspire.
Reading Nozick reminds me.
I never believed
I belonged to the world—wrote
A string of suicide notes.


Twice-told beggarman—
Is this why I've stayed out of
Politics so long?
Am I a hypocrite now
To join the conversation?

Nozick, Shapiro,
Vallicella—do any
Of these people know
How it is to survive for
A one-eyed, three-legged dog?


I still haven't put
The books back on the shelf I
Fixed some weeks ago.
Papers cover the sofa.
Who'll get this mess when I die?


Austin Osman Spare
Declared a bat grows its wings
Through unconscious will.
I fear, being too conscious,
This bat—I mean I—won't fly.


### 30<sup>th</sup> November (Thursday)

Many would-be moths
And butterflies end life as
Cocoons—stillreborn.
I liquefy, but have I
Left it too late to pupate?

When will I become
Someone? When will I attain
Being? Never. So
I might as well carry on
With this MA—pass or fail.


You don't know how things
Are on the ground—we rely
On stretched volunteers.
A better world? First drum up
Demand. Do you have contacts?


At the end, perhaps,
He envisaged the complete
Disintegration
Of his life's work. He was right.
That's what 'life' and
'work'—twinned—mean.


Before the final
Judge I'll stand a mere lover,
Failed, inadequate.
"This is all I am." Into
Nothing's lap: "Take me! Take me!"

In the post, inscribed:
"To the new guardian of
This book, till the next."
*Folktales of Japan*. First owned
By one Venetia Newell.


They weren't in the bar
Where they said they'd be. I left
For home. Sparse, chill rain.
At the lights, hot dog smells cross
To me. They always tempt me.

# DECEMBER
*(2018)*

## 1st December (Saturday)


I have no silence.
If it were an old record
That had become scratched
I could buy a new copy,
But it's the world that is scratched.


At four seventeen
I alighted in Erith
Not knowing whether
I'd reach the Town Hall in time.
I found the place near empty.


In year-end darkness,
The office for taxi hire,
Shops with wigs on heads.
I wish I could cut this loose
To drift into forever.

Better, much better
By far than all those models
Of ultimate truth
That instead have cut off God
From all we hear, see and touch.


And year-end darkness
Could be the world's end. I wish.
If only it could,
By ending, slay that dragon
Of fear, of science—Future.


A simple statement:
I have respect for, look to,
Christianity.
And yet it manufactures
Atheists, by exclusion.


To destroy oneself,
To annihilate oneself,
To die to oneself,
Is the narrow path to good.
Like so, to love one's neighbour.

The world *worlds* (noun, verb),
According to Heidegger.
I freely concur.
But can A.I. ever world?
Do its makers even world?


## 2nd December (Sunday)


To be able to
Spend whole days just ordering
My own library,
Like someone who's lived through war,
Who dies into history.


One's prime meant wholeness,
I thought. And in those prime days
Burned with conviction
That the truth could not be heard
And disbelieved. Changes came.


Countless as seashells.
Plastic tops, unscrewable,
Pluggable, with spouts,
For squeezy bottles. What if
Each of these were carved by hand?

Lydon once opined
The Queen had made us morons,
But isn't it clear
Who the culprit is today?
Rotten, vicious—our new roots.


### 3rd December (Monday)

A house is a world.
Remembering 10 Heath Street.
Has Pete moved again?
The Green Man guards the cellar.
Coffee on mornings-after.


Visiting, these days,
And in London—it's not like
How I remember.
We didn't appreciate
How much this country would change.


Perhaps in ten years,
Or thirty, we'll look back on
Those warm sitting rooms,

As rich as Christmas pudding,
As we do ruined abbeys.


Ah, the dreadful things
I've done, suicides threatened.
I shook someone's hand
On one occasion, after
I'd just vomited on mine.


Coming off Facebook
For the Christmas period,
I find solitude
Bringing the world back to me,
And glad anticipation.


I disconnected
The house phone this very day.
I've had nothing but
Cold calls and scammers for months.
And now the handset has died.


Watching my father
Interviewed, I see how much
I've hidden myself
From people—barbarians
Of sanity, everywhere.

### 4th December (Tuesday)

The problems linger
Like shadows cast by objects
You no longer see.
The sun mellows in the west
And the shadows lengthen, spread.


Thrown into the midst
Of this endless cornering
Where ivy stretches,
Luxuriant and given,
And freedom is to give in.


### 5th December (Wednesday)

This tinnitus, like
A broken machine I can't
Turn off—stand-by whine.
This tintinnabulation
Travestying Arvo Pärt.

No caller ID
From whoever phoned during
The seminar. Odd.
Anxious, I dial 'messages'.
It's Erith Town Hall. Of course!


I often prefer
Intercourse (no, not sexual)
With the dead. And why?
Because they seem more alive
Than today's woke sleepwalkers.


How to throw off these
Festering fetters without
The inanity
Of rebelling? To reach out?
To withdraw? Simply, to be?


I remind myself
Sometimes that—for example—
At least for the length
Of this train journey, no one
Can get to me too badly.

A text I've just sent:
"Funny how simple language
Can be the grandest:
'. . . the things that come to be and
Pass away.'" From Al-Kindī.


They would scorn the thought,
Our overlords (scientists,
I mean), of someone
Appearing out of nothing.
But the universe? Brute fact.


Why did God make me?
Only that people might know
The peculiar
Laughter of sexless freedom.
And a puzzling sadness.


### 6<sup>th</sup> December (Thursday)


It's simply assumed
That I should be complicit.
Everyone I meet—

Ah, the loathsomeness of it!—
Makes me co-conspirator.


The last three arches
In the corner are profuse
With leaves and berries,
As if just here a stony
Spring broke out, made patterns, froze.


### 7<sup>th</sup> December (Friday)

The BBC. Strange
How clear it is to me now—
I fall quite outside
The glow of those they include
In the safe, right-thinking 'we'.


In the lecture, she
Told us, suddenly, how bad
The Christians had been,
How open the Muslim world.
No choice but to let it pass.

Someone who never
Used to like Doctor Who now
Loves it. Why? Because
It supports diversity.
Is this all that's left for us?


Sometimes, now, I have
This dream. I stand on trial
Before all my friends.
"Guilty," I say, "if this be
A crime. It's time—erase me."


Computer repairs.
Laptops from forty-nine pounds.
Our miraculous
Devastation, like the night,
Holds this cubbyhole of light.


From the beginning
I hated Tim Minchin. Then
Saw his support for
Enforcing the vote. Evil
Leered beneath the eyeliner.

## 8ᵗʰ December (Saturday)


Eschatology—
That full-stop to human time—
Was one of those things
I could not live with. Strange how
It's become habitable.


As if human time
Is its own country. We may
Cross the border, but
The border can't expand. We're
Buried here or emigrate.


What have we done? We
Must look at it, as someone
Who is dying must
Face death. Why must we? Is there
In that 'must' some kind of hope?


I see even in
This tree with curled leaves clinging
The beginning of
A gentle apocalypse
In the mode of a novel.

## 9<sup>th</sup> December (Sunday)

Ivory tower.
A pejorative term. Yet
It's quiet up here
And you can see, centuries
Away, other towers, lit.


Is it possible
That God doesn't get these jokes
By which we make space
And context to breathe meaning?
God, on whom all this depends?


I was born during
A long peace, but soon enough
Normal service is
To be resumed. Unfinished
Business of apocalypse.


There's no audience
For me except the hopeless
Human race. Can I

Contribute constructively
To something wholly debased?


From a single piece
Of ivory these towers
Have been carved. Their source?
The tusk of an elephant
On whose back the world rested.


Look down to the plain
Below these towers and see
Volcanic flowers
Bloom and blacken. What a view!
History itself ablaze.


The local council
Seem only to desire
That the earth's surface
Should be rendered as barren
As our cratered satellite.


So the Last Judgement,
I seem to see, is a fount
Eternal, leaping
In each moment with colours
Of unique revelation.

I'm in a dark place.
No one will find me. I see
Them pass. They knew me
For years, yet not one of them
Noticed that I disappeared.


## 10<sup>th</sup> December (Monday)

The best of both worlds—
If I didn't exist. First,
The world would exist.
(I'm no Atlas.) And second,
It would be like it didn't.


This is one of those
Eerie periods. Songs and
Fairy lights suggest
The never of what should but
Can't be, smearing everything.


We're here because we're
Here because we're here because

We're here. So it is
Mere existence corresponds,
Cries out, to crucifixion.


Unless we accept
The good of crucifixion,
The cross as tent pole
Of existence, we must side
With Julio Cabrera.


### 11<sup>th</sup> December (Tuesday)


"They don't want standards,"
Aickman lamented. Always
This friction between
The masses and the elite;
Loyalties switch, depending.


As if this life is
A party thrown for me, not
Necessarily
Welcome. I give what I can,
Waiting to be left alone.

The adverts that might
Still have been aimed at me, now
Just could never be.
See how the world falls away.
But I've been somewhat prepared.


### 12<sup>th</sup> December (Wednesday)


Living alone. We
Know this reduces life-span.
Yet it's required
For reasons of work. Frankly,
Some of us just deserve it.


This is how worthless
I am: I always only
Wanted to create
A sense of magic, live with
Others within it; I failed.


I failed because
I am too weak. The others
Were more convincing.
"This is the world," they said. "This!
Everything is politics."

I'm wondering why
I should care. No one tells me.
No one can. To save
Myself from Hell? Is that all?
Let me watch bats as day dies.


You hit it, it rings.
Numerically distinct. One
Human life. You can
Never understand because
It's just as full as yours is.


So I can't compare
The value of my studies
With what's come before.
I sink in the infinite,
Whether it be theirs or mine.


The end of the year.
Travelling through sleeves of cold
To pockets of warmth,
Buttoned by windows and doors.
Here my smarting hands expand.

From my notes: "Moderns
*Become*. Ancients *be*. The line
And the circle." Where
Do we think the line will go?
The terminus blazes, cracks.


### 13<sup>th</sup> December (Thursday)

I've borrowed thousands
To lift myself out of this
Swamp I've been stuck in,
By the boot-strap pulley of
Philosophy. Please let me.


The field of battle
Was vast. I was lost in it.
Now it has shrunk to
A mere chessboard, few pieces
Left on it, checkmate in sight.


All the holy truths
We have contested over
Centuries. Again,

And in a new form, we must
Harrow out the heresies.


## 14th December (Friday)


The holy words that
Animate the maelstrom
Of current currents:
'Innocent victim'. We must
Learn to separate the two.


Everything but me
(I think, walking through the mall)
Is God. Everything
Is doomed. I wish I were doomed
With God and with everything.


Only mineral
And plastic. Lights reflect from
Glossy surfaces.
This is what the savage blood
Of history was shed for.

It's your fault you're not
Elon Musk. It's your fault you're
Not Beyoncé Knowles.
The damp hopelessness of it
As buses pass in the cold.


The desolate years
Spent journeying, all the rooms
And human strangeness,
Just for one startling hour, words
From a friend about to leave.


### 15<sup>th</sup> December (Saturday)

When I was little
More than a child I believed
Self-imposed exile
Would make me a prophet. No.
It's only made me vagrant.


How long? Another
Thirty years—forty?—of this
Ringing in my ears?

Its source is inside me now.
How accidental life is.


Why is it my 'no'
Doesn't mean 'no'? Others are
Treated as adults
Who know their own minds. No one
Will ever believe I work.


At some point, the rope
That frays will snap. At some point,
The weight will exceed
The grip. The push, at some point,
Will push right through. Then we fall.


## 16<sup>th</sup> December (Sunday)

The most effective
Route to misanthropy? Try
Pleasing everyone.
The whole grasping wrangle turns
Incandescent with lightning.

They push from one side;
They push from the other. They
Hate the centrists. They
Hate each other. It's hard just
To stand up straight and resist.


How I remember
The cathartic glory of
Those old songs: "Fuck you,
Fuck you, fuck you, one and all!"
My adolescence shines through.


### 17<sup>th</sup> December (Monday)

Populism. They
Hate it when it doesn't go
Their way. Yet it's what
They breathe and speak, the same beat
Heard at every house party.


This season is like
A war. I don't know if I'll
Complete my mission,

But each card written, gift sent,
Is one more enemy down.


I wish you could know
How besieged I feel. If you
Reach out to a snail
It tends to recoil. Keep still.
Wait. I might extend myself.


I met John, by chance,
Exiting Foyle's. "It must mean
Something," he said. Yes,
But what? I will remember
When I'm dying. And that's what.


### 18th December (Tuesday)


There are certain things
Only years will make you see.
Youth tugs indignant
And excited at the sleeves
Of age—those sleeves are his skin.

A weakness of mine—
That I am no ascetic.
Weaknesses combine
And have tailored for me this
Permanent aural cilice.


Jordan Peterson
Defends Christianity,
Hates nihilism.
Are they different? Adherents
Of both wait on the world's end.


What normality
Of worldly meanings is it
Most people live in,
Between touching poles? Children's
Voices tell me I've missed it.


Strange how I always
Knew I was a ghost. Something
To be ashamed of,
Until I find my way home
To the night's most haunted blue.

Not much longer left
For me, to walk among trees
And twilight and rain
And watch the country die while
Buses pass by, to Thamesmead.


When I find my place,
My desk facing the evening,
Forever-windowed,
The view by J.A. Grimshaw,
I'll pen ghost stories, and dream.


## 19<sup>th</sup> December (Wednesday)

To have a catch-up—
As if all souls decided,
"Let's split up and see
What we can find." Billions
In web-linked meanwhile sagas.


I want time to dream.
How carefully, on a dig,
The excavations
Are made. Soft brushes remove
Dust. I'd take such care with dreams.

No one else knows—not
As quickly and with such pain—
When I'm on fire.
I shouldn't just raise my hand
And wait for them to notice.


### 20<sup>th</sup> December (Thursday)

Parents and children
Must fight, since children want not
What they want, but rules.
How weary it makes me. I'm
Alone because I won't fight.


I was told: no need
To fill in that form. Then, that
I had a month. Then
(Before then, actually), my
Benefit was suspended.

I am once again
What I was: a knotted stick.
A twisted branch was
Chosen by the carver's whim.
How change? My pain is my shape.


"Consistency is
The fetish of small minds." I
Disagree. Since it
Must be inclusive, it draws
Us on to wider vistas.


I tried the door. Locked.
An organ? Anyway, sounds.
Then, "Were you looking
For me?" The new vicar. I
Explained I was just passing.


She welcomed me in.
I wanted to see, I said,
The mural. Who was
That king? Aethelberht? The pews
Were decked out with Christmas trees.

**21$^{st}$ December (Friday)**

It's my habit when
I hear the usual cant from
Public atheists
To look up whether they have
Children. Yes? They're in bad faith.

**22$^{nd}$ December (Saturday)**

I think of those words
Of Peter's, meant to explain
A clash of thoughts: "You're
Just at different places." Some
Places I will never go.


Some places I have
Been to and will not go back.
Disconsolately
I look round and learn that such
Are the places most call home.

Most of this discourse
Seems to me motivated
By ill-will. If they
Only did evil, it would
Speak for itself. Worse, they lie.


How scared should we be?
How scared do you want to be?
Maybe I've taken
Things too lightly, but at least
I've forced life on nobody.


## 23rd December (Sunday)


I woke before six.
To travel, that is, to be
Leaving somewhere, this
Makes my morning footsteps ring.
Departure: Mishima's muse.


Wrong turns in history,
Number fifty-seven: they
Didn't ban phone calls
On trains in Britain before
People could form the habit.

At Kidbrooke Station
The train pauses. Adjacent
High-risers show their
Corners to the track, one wrapped
In tarpaulin, a box-kite.


We're expected to
Have opinions on things we
Know nothing about,
And yet they're never welcome.
As if people *want* to fight.


A man with white hair,
Carrying an umbrella,
Comes down the steps of
His house, on Ashburnham Road—
A twig on history's tree.


On the seat in front,
On the coach, a young man holds
A video game
And jerks like a stiff fish hooked
On a tugged-tight line of dream.

Layer on layer
Of rain as the coach rolls on
Towards Barnstaple.
The roadside vegetation
Used to hint; now it conjures.


## 24th December (Monday)


The seventies film,
*Scrooge*—of the faces, for me,
Only one or two
Were familiar. How strange
An actor's fate—Rent-a-ghost.


Life will be renewed,
But I won't. It's this we find
Difficult. Are we
Most essentially that snake,
Life, or the skin that it sheds?


Love is not only
An act of will, or I would
Have willed it. There must
Be an authenticating
Fact, which comes first, and I lack.

Of five siblings, I
Was the one who took on
The heirloom of decay.
There it lay among the deeds
And keys. I feared it, and grabbed.

## 25<sup>th</sup> December (Tuesday)

Visiting, I am
Reacquainted with T.V.
Judging purely by
What's broadcast, all reason to
Love my homeland is now gone.

I could read, I'm sure,
A hagiography of
Robert Smith, and when
I catch a lift, enthuse re
All the things I never knew.

Are these the only
Means I have for growing old

Without despair? Masks
To hide despair are themselves
Despair. Sickness unto death.


Like condensation,
My thoughts evaporating
As I grow older.
I will observe them as if
A meteorologist.


Imagine, as in
The films, an electronic
Super mind began
To read—to read everything.
This might well be enchantment.


## 26th December (Wednesday)


I try to relate
This age to that. There must be
Hidden seeds for such
Results. And the soil forms
Layers—strange, almost distinct.

There are those of us
Who were not born to keep house
Alone, nor to have
Servants, nor to keep house with
Another, who might love us.


Only another
Five hundred million years
Till the Earth becomes
Uninhabitable. We
Might as well pack up our kit.


I boil the kettle
For hot water to shave with.
I'm as decrepit
As this house is. Even my
Untrimmed eyebrows wax frowzy.


### 27<sup>th</sup> December (Thursday)


The central heating
Is working once again. That
Sound. Something greater

Than oneself. That's what I want
To become when I pass on.


The hopelessness is
Mixed up with normality.
It's hard to believe
In that far, bright star. Yet all
We've made is steeped in its light.


The same handwriting,
The familiar squeezy
Bottle of honey,
Conversion chart. All these things
As if they are forever.


## 28th December (Friday)


I don't know why I
Should be sorry. More and more
I understand war.
These appeasing fools will squeeze
Us into mass suicide.

Would life be quiet,
Running a bus-station caff?
Perhaps not. Quiet
Is always elsewhere. What's sure:
The man serving says little.


England is tiresome
And has grown feeble besides.
Yet worst of all: her
Sons and daughters hate her and
Wallow in their matricide.


Consider the task
Of the choirmaster, tending
The fast-dimming fire.
Choirboys hide behind tombstones,
Scared to be seen near the church.


Along the High Street,
I hoped some altered face might
Recognise me. None
Did. Such stillness. Nightfall. Smoke
Drifted over the graveyard.


Private memory,
The coach-window reflection:

Bare branches road-map
Darkening skies. These churches,
Though preserved, won't multiply.


Lights out on the coach
Favours the back-lit screen, not
Printed page. That faint
Voice, "Remember, remember,"
Stirs the half-buried embers.


## 29th December (Saturday)


Little incidents
That make up most of life. At
Some airport, my bag
Was inadequate, old. My
Brother bought me a new one.


My housing has been
Uncertain. Friends have offered
Me a room. Gladness.
Though I don't know if I can
Take it, my fall feels broken.

## 30th December (Sunday)

On the Gravesend train.
Someday I'll go all the way
To the terminus.
In the meantime I must keep
My thoughts mostly to myself.


Why must I hold back?
Others freely noise about
Their safe little hates.
Sometimes I even smile. They'd
Be surprised at my targets.


That scumbag, Turing,
That dripping, unctuous fraud,
Stewart Lee. God, why
Must I forever merely
Nod politely at such names?


But, as Descartes says,
There is no hate without some
Sadness. How tainted

This world is. But why approve
Some hatreds and ban others?


There'll come a time when
Either I must get down on
My knees and pray, or
Stand up and face what's coming
To me. Censure? Torture? Love?


### 31ˢᵗ December (Monday)


The worst part of this
Internet addiction is
When I've been away
And come back, I find I've missed
Nothing. And yet it goes on.


My router broke down
Just yesterday. Deadlines loom.
Essays. And beyond,
Royalties to calculate.
Always the threat of disgrace.

And homelessness, and
My being a parasite,
And misogynist.
An oppressor, says the left.
But a weakling, says the right.


Why dwell on all this
When I stand forever at
The threshold of death?
When I exit unnoticed,
For goodbye I'll smile and sigh.

# JANUARY
*(2019)*

**1ˢᵗ January (Tuesday)**

I woke late. The words
'Universal credit' were
The first on my mind.
This reform is like a purge.
God knows if I'll survive it.


An image takes form
In my mind with clarity—
A balancing sheet.
On one side, reasons to live.
I must fill it in with care.


Besieged. Benefit
Suspended. Flat up for sale.
Deadlines impendent.
No sail on the horizon.
No word from reinforcements.

White berries on twigs
Without leaf. Withered bushes.
We approach the gate.
The marble-grey New Year skies
Make visible voiceless dread.


They don't even know
There are people such as we
To be considered.
We've never existed, so
Our passing won't be noticed.


I feel myself slide
Down a narrow well, round wall
Smooth and slippery.
As I sink deeper, my voice
Grows weaker; air, light, thinner.


To be forced to choose
Between life and death: life shoves
One way; death shoves back.
Which will shove hardest? We don't
Yet know. We must hope it's death.

Nightfall is still swift.
I take socks and underwear
From the oil heater.
I take down the calendars.
A walk, then quiet reading.


What fantastic grey
Canopy is this, so low
Above the houses?
As if to keep in the spell
Of mere vacancy, it hangs.


## 2nd January (Wednesday)


There's not the interest
To sustain these projects. Lives
That start badly strain
Through a long losing streak in
The game of Monopoly.


On a larger scale,
Isn't this the position
Of the human race?
Borrowing from this side, then
That—a doomed balancing act.

I, who must borrow,
Find it hard to lend. And we,
Each borrowing from
Borrowers, try to slow our
Mutual, long-term descent.


After the review
I am forty pounds a month
Worse off. One by one
They prise from this cruel edge my
Fingers, till their job is done.


"You're looking good," she
Says. I can tell she means it.
Battered, crushed, driven
Close to laughter, I'm intrigued:
Do rough winds, then, make us glow?


I take a rest. On
The threshold of sleep, I smell
The faint, noble scent
Of a candle, realise
How whole and at home I am.

The changes afoot
Could wipe me clean away. I
Look ahead with dread,
As to an execution.
The end. No retribution.


### 3rd January (Thursday)


Last night's foreboding—
What was it? I've gambled on
Winning in good time.
Now the time I've gambled with
Is over. Debts are called in.


What chips can I cash?
I've gambled away any
Chance of love or home.
Strange to pray to Fortune's Wheel
Again. "Luck, please don't crush me!"


Frankenstein's monster,
Parts pilfered from the graveyard
Of embarrassment.
That's what I am. I must stoop
Defiantly before fate.

And fame, that thing I
Once wanted? The internet
Displays its virtues.
What would it be for me but
To surf a cannibal crowd?


Materialists
Tend to be determinists,
But think about it.
Are we saying that Ken Dodd
Was just inevitable?


Something about, "You're
Not depressed; you're surrounded
By arseholes." That quote.
Well, surrounded-by-arseholes
Is the internet effect.


Half past five. Grey trees
Bring back the old dream: flitting
Free like evening's ghost.
But money worries rack each
Scene. Trapped, because embodied.

Let's get behind this.
What do we really believe
Procreation's for?
To populate a dying
Universe? Play Judgement Day?


### 4ᵗʰ January (Friday)

I don't understand
These complex tariffs. I don't
Have the time to look
At the factors behind this
Backache. Lone, I muddle through.


I'm not one of those
Who designed this world, therefore
It is not designed
For me, and so my chances
Of designing are kept low.


Not masculine or
Feminine, no. I feel like
The man in the moon
If the moon were a balloon
Full of mystical gayness.

I feel so stranded,
I only occasionally
Try to explain it.
See the tail of my Q?—that's
The string of the blue balloon.


This blue gay balloon,
How has it survived? Till now
It's been protected
By the fearsome statues of
A blood-shamed, fagged-out empire.


Voices—living, dead,
Forever jeering. "You know
Nothing!" Then, when I
Try to learn: "The sin of pride!"
Give me a hand, you bastards.


### 5<sup>th</sup> January (Saturday)


It's forbidden for
Non-Christians to find meaning
In the crucifix?
If so, how will they ever
Be attracted from outside?

Boundary policing—
That's what they call it—the strange
Upkeep of the group.
"You've come this close, so, are you
Friend or foe? Get in, or go!"


I might never come
Closer than this—close enough
Just to go to Hell.
Liberalism fails; misfits
Like me are default quislings.


Yet I understand,
More and more, how essential
Is group loyalty.
From anarchy, tyranny;
I weaken society.


Yet to have only
Groups is to have only war.
Retire from the field.
We must look into these things,
Each in religious detail.

## 6<sup>th</sup> January (Sunday)

I'm someone who is
Too polite. I pretend not
To know what I know,
Just to please those people who
Choose to believe in evil.


I read of Schlegel's
Bubbling infinity.
That's just how it seems
To me. Strange how people find
This offensive. They've been hurt.


But I've been hurt, too,
By their hurt. I know how to
Give them what they want.
Here, more doom, more hatred. Please,
Can I have my pension now?


I know well enough
I could die this very month.
I know no one else

Will know how to read my words.
I must lay out labelled keys.


These fragments are knots
In eternity's net. Bound,
Embodied, by which
We know the unknowable:
Infinite interstices.


How did it happen
That, for me, the early Cure
Came to inhabit
A place of memory and
Magic beyond all questions?


### 7<sup>th</sup> **January (Monday)**

The monster behind
The curtain in the forest.
The toad by the pond.
I still know these places, though
I tread them less frequently.

Sacred is secret.
No one has ever seen that
Boy with chestnut hair.
I tried to make him live, till
I knew he must be hidden.


I think of Harry,
With his stories and guitars.
Seagull afternoons.
He laughed, "I'm old. You can't just
Keep saying you're middle-aged."


No one ever crossed
My threshold, dived in that pond,
Drew back that curtain.
There are many cleverer
Than me, but some things I see.


### 8th January (Tuesday)


Blindsided. Driven
Off the road. Concentration
Reduced to pedals

And steering wheel. All other
Processes shut down for now.


During the winter,
This flat settles deep into
A world of moisture.
I get used to it like one
Too cold to change his clothing.


A most wonderful
Mystery—I mean it—is
This gladness to be
Alive, which I feel knowing
My armpits are just inflamed.


### 9th January (Wednesday)


You must know the rules
Before you break them, they say.
A sound principle.
I must learn reality,
Then to fantasy return.

I've quite a backlog
Of unpublished work. I could
Concentrate on that.
Shovel it out steadily
Into the trough where none feed.


Outside at The Rose,
Five women round a table.
Finger-chilling wind.
I pass and notice the scent
Of make-up and tobacco.


## 10<sup>th</sup> January (Thursday)

The fact that Kate Bush
Felt the need to clarify
Her comments on May—
How weary it makes me. How
Indescribably weary.


Just the normal stress
Of living. You sense faintly
The fact that humans
Could easily lynch you and
Sell photos of your charred corpse.

People forever
Symbolically perform what
At some level they
Remember—inquisitions,
Wars, purges—keep rehearsing.


Is it because we're
Creatures of the land that we're
Surprised when life shows
Itself unstable? Do fish
Care that the seas are rising?


One grows tired of it.
Telling the expected lies,
Hating the people
On the official hate list.
Do none of you own mirrors?


The desert's sacred
Riddle. Arid lifelessness.
But rain calls blooms from
Hidden seeds. Such as this, too,
Is human society.

## 11ᵗʰ **January (Friday)**

Objects in this flat—
This flat only rented—
Are like time condensed.
Like moments of time, solid
On shelves, until I'm moved on.


Cold air limns my shins.
I think of Benatar's list
Of why life is bad.
"Thermal discomfort." That was
The one that stuck in my mind.


Time moves, so we feel
We must, too. Deadlines loom. We
Must gather money.
But what's wrong with here? This? If
Only we could find repose.


Here. Opaque. I speak
A language without knowing
How language arose.

This nest is I and not-I,
This home, an alien world.


Both despair and hope,
Thinking of that ratio:
World to attention.
My efforts will not be saved,
And science will not prevail.


## 12th January (Saturday)


There have been people
Who were humble and aimed high,
Star-gazing. Today
It's the reverse. People aim
At the dirt and self-promote.


There's much in my life
To regret. Guideless, I have
Wasted so much time
On junk that there's little time
Left to indulge in regret.

There are people who
Think it's enough just to die.
They die too soon, leave
Shallow suicide notes. Am
I still too much in a rush?


So arrogantly
Innocent, they can't conceive
Others are just as
Offended as they are, by
Different things, and keep quiet.


Rather than doing,
Dreaming is far sweeter, but
Leaves me as I am.
So I hesitate to own
My beatific idleness.


The chamber music
Of eternity awaits
All who close their eyes
And listen. But to join in?
That secret remains hidden.

## 13th January (Sunday)

Exodus. "But God,
You said if we fled Egypt,
We would find our home."
On and on and on I roam,
God's only words: "Keep going."


I have seen night fall
More often by far than I
Have seen the day dawn.
Both crepuscules are profound;
Why the excess of sundown?


This one-sided life
We live, knowing funerals
Never as death's bride.
One by one they leave us, to
Marry, leave us bridesmaids all.

## 14th January (Monday)

The most obvious
Sign that we're not in control:
We will surely die.
A paradox, some say. No.
Faith is only common sense.


Only a matter
Of time until we depart
From time, whatever
That means. A strange certainty
Beneath this uncertainty.


Short days nonetheless
Incline my mind westerly
To eternity's
Horizon. I seem to see
A suburb there, windows lit.


Inside that final
Curve, the universe's rim,
The darkness outside,
Light within, one kotatsu,
Warm; someone to share it with.

When you're drifting in
Space, it's hard to control your
Direction. Those with
An interest in the future
Link hands. Others drift away.


## 15<sup>th</sup> January (Tuesday)

There are three things now
I think when I wake up and
When I go to bed:
I'm tired, I'm alone and I'm
Financially insecure.


It's strange that age must
Execute the plans drawn up
By a vanished child.
Sacrifices, he foresaw;
Not that there'd be no reward.


Still, I'm left with this
Curious plan, gone cold though
Semi-audacious.
Examining it I find
Marks of blind integrity.

No one looks. No one
Sees. Instead they wait in place,
Sea anemones.
They grasp at that on which they
Will feed. Blindly—each other.


I was just enough
Of the rough to shrug and guess
Someone might miss me.
Well, I've learnt that trick, but not
The nerve to say, "Stick with me."


### 16<sup>th</sup> January (Wednesday)

There's a kind of love
You only catch glimpses of.
It guides you on. Kant's
Reason went before him. He
Was buried with due honour.


So much depends on
Memory. Dimly we sense

Two lovers once vowed
Not to forget, but time's vast
Perspectives swallowed them up.


Eternity is
The bridegroom, Time, the bride. Where
They touch is weeping
Made of every meeting and
Goodbye. How can we bear it?


Did someone look at
Me thirty years back and think,
"Bloody hell, if I'm
Not careful I'll get lynched!"? There
Comes the thought of high windows.


### 17<sup>th</sup> January (Thursday)


I don't like meeting
People much anymore. Why?
Maybe two reasons:
They think they can read your mind.
They think that they're the police.

How did I suppress
My thoughts and feelings all those
Years? I'll tell you how:
Exactly how I am now,
Just with a different window.


All the people I
Have to be polite to. All
The friends I might lose.
All the blame I have to take
For rumours, lies and mistakes.


Condensation blurs
The lights of pre-dawn traffic.
Time to meditate.
I open my eyes. Daylight
Has raised the wreck of my room.


Jim Davidson, I
Never liked, but I sometimes
Remember those words:
"What am I meant to do? Curl
Up and die?" Yes. So am I.

## 18ᵗʰ January (Friday)

Let me take you on
A journey. You might like it,
Or perhaps you won't.
Watch how this fey shoe-gazer
Became a dodgy geezer.


Just something meta:
I composed that last poem
Yesterday, then thought
Better of including it,
But this morning I'm quite dry.


Male fragility.
"I thought you right-wingers were
Supposed to be tough."
All that stuff. But I've never
Thought I was strong. Or right-wing.


Instead it's the left
Who are thugs, who are bullies,
Who lust for power,
Who can't take criticism,
Can't take *this* criticism.

It's like I've swallowed
Poison but am not allowed
To vomit. At least
Let me vomit, or else just
Prove what poisoners you are.


Everyone wants me
To take sides, so everyone
Pushes me away.
You'll be surprised when I'm pushed,
At last, into judging you.


### 19<sup>th</sup> January (Saturday)


When Winston Smith says
He hates everything good, I
Recognise his plight.
They define themselves as good,
So, then, I must be evil.


It's as if, in war,
They cried "unfair" when they saw

That their foes were armed.
"Bad guys don't have the right to
Self-defence." I fell for it.


The conversation
We had last night has made me
See. What irony!
I long to please the group, yet
There's no group where I belong.


I can't just unbe.
Is an apology and
A promise enough?
I'm sorry, and I promise
One day I'll be gone for good.


### 20<sup>th</sup> January (Sunday)

Don't meet anyone,
Don't talk to anyone, or
If you must, simply
Agree with them. Keep yourself
To yourself. Pay your way. Die.

Pre-nup, work pension,
Mortgage, cohabitation,
Respect from your peers,
The next step in your career.
These things lie beyond my sphere.


Since I'm a dead end,
Don't talk to me; let me be
A mere voyeur. See
The grand desolation writ
In city lights just for me.


The operation:
I will learn who my friends are
By setting boundaries,
By telling the truth instead
Of what is just expected.


### 21<sup>st</sup> January (Monday)

My strange exclusion
From sexual affirmation
Is transcendental.

It doesn't exist; that I
Exist presupposes it.


Existing can't be
Illegal, they say. Well, soon
It will be for me.
Of all their hypocrisies
This might be the master key.


Yet again last night
I let a friend express his
Views aggressively.
I politely signalled I
Might demur; I was ignored.


Panentheism
Comes under criticism,
With fine distinctions.
"We must be careful." What? To
Seize the deeds to God's estate?


I am a snowflake.
I always was. Bring out your
Blowtorch, Warrior!
Or, since wyrd angels told me
I'm a heartflower, pluck me.

We live in the world
Of If, the conditioned. (If
I publish, I'm damned.)
There is something before If,
And this is what we call God.


Since I'll be soon gone,
What good thing have I done? I've
Read Horace Walpole.
I've dipped my finger in that
Pool and watched the ripples grow.


I will die. All I
Tried to be, untouchable;
All I was, reversed.
Before that great joy, just let
Me read MacDonald's *Phantastes*.


### 22<sup>nd</sup> January (Tuesday)


It's not that I think
I'm a good person. I'm just
Not far-gone enough

To place my weaknesses in
Their hands and say, "Here you are!"


We're called to confess
By people who want only
To diminish us.
Why should I feel guilty when
'It's all power relations'?


A bright winter's day.
On the platform lampposts wear
P.A. speakers like
Pairs of bells. Simplicity
Might yet let us start again.


Citizen's Advice.
They were down to two staff, like
That sad ratio:
Conscience to sin. They had no
Choice but to turn me away.


Because it has snowed
I miss you. Is that strange? I
Recall with a jolt
We can't share warmth as we did.
I stop myself from phoning.

## 23rd January (Wednesday)

For me this flat is
A conjuring trick. Hard to
Set up; worse is this:
A rug unrolls with tea-things;
Now I must roll it back up.


Hypertension, yes,
And inflammation, back ache,
Tinnitus, cricked neck.
It's easy to believe that
The not-yet best is never.


Even to mention
That stupid ad drags us down,
And I can't think this:
Those who liked it are brain-washed.
But they'll think worse about me.


It's a commonplace
To say you only notice
Things when they are gone.

I notice the consensus
It seems no longer exists.


To live is to die.
Words by Cliff Burton, though cribbed
Partly from elsewhere.
To lie is to kill some piece
Of the world. What now survives?


As babyhood is
Closer to birth, so am I
To death—death's infant.
Building blocks and see-saws, but
With bones, alas, more brittle.


Learning history,
Listening to Mick Ronson,
Make me want to stay.
Dealing with estate agents
Makes me long for my last day.


In darkness it's not
Clear which are the paths and which
Just gaps between trees.
Then let the darkness descend
So we can stray, holding hands.

I have a soft spot
For evil. That's why I'm not
Sure we should die out.
If you're a Calvinist, say,
Or Buddhist, why have children?


Each time we meet might
Be without 'again', and we
Might even know this.
Yet, look: life states, "I am of
An endless line the latest."


### 24<sup>th</sup> January (Thursday)


In those days, leaving
Was always agony. Why?
No one would notice
My attempts to say goodbye.
In fact, the pattern lingers.


Yet these things I do
Out of politeness. I would

Far rather simply
Get up and leave. Always this
Asymmetry troubles me.


Piano music
And a furnished room evoke
A sense of the world
As an extended headland
Of named things. Resting on what?


## 25th January (Friday)


The seriousness
Of death is something we want
To capture. But why?
I say you'll probably be
Okay—'probably' wobbles.


Always far away,
The strict limit of all we
See: the horizon.
But your centre will pass that
Circumference. Awe is fitting.

## 26ᵗʰ January (Saturday)

It's clear I never
Wanted to be known. When I
Talk too much I feel
Degraded, no matter what
I've said. I have no place here.


Nostalgia extends
To food. The hotpot bubbles.
We got through winter
On such fare. I ate it with
Others; I ate it alone.


So strange. Not only
That your access to me will
Run out, but also
That you yourself will lose your
Is. How did time become us?

## 27ᵗʰ January (Sunday)


Having recently
Arrived, you might conclude not
Much is going on.
You don't understand the long
History of this island.


As your years amass,
The backstory takes up more
Time, grows more complex.
You're absorbed in a drama
Like four-dimensional chess.


So much condensed in
The last acts; the need and time
To advertise shrink.
Often your asides are lost
On the few who stop to watch.


Here on this island,
Taller than it is wide, see
The crags and the falls.
Some species are found only
Here. Some words. Some festivals.

## 28th January (Monday)

Could it be we will
Return our tricked attention
To our relation
With infinity, scorning
The cruel limits of machine?


## 29th January (Tuesday)

The lies are simpler
And easier to repeat,
So we have a choice:
Collude with ignorance or
Risk becoming elitist.


The modern world is
Sentimental. Feelings, not
Principles, hold sway.
Is it right that I'm going
To Hell? In principle, yes.

Robots of virtue.
They're not sad; they're not happy.
They do the right thing.
It's of interest to no one.
Does my defensiveness show?


### 30ᵗʰ January (Wednesday)


What was it like for
Tolkien to get a letter
From a fan who was
Also Princess Margrethe?
Was it like calling to like?


The shelves, endless shelves
Of books behind talking heads,
Can't be contained in
Shot, or life. So life escapes
Itself in dream furniture.

Beyond the scraggly
Black of trees, the sky, as clear
As a mirror, though
Reflecting clouds, stretches light's
Sweet ache. Death, wait till the spring.


## 31st January (Thursday)


This flat, with lights on,
Books everywhere, as day ends.
Time and mind grow stark.
Time will run out. I almost
Grasp how the contrast casts mind.


Music videos
Are the lowest form of art.
Lowness was freedom.
They're now revered, though they've lost
Their freedom and gained nothing.


Stealthily I scout
The frozen highlands where I
Feel I don't belong.
Scavenge the beaten lowlands
For what freedom there remains.

'Metamorphosis'
By Philip Glass. Fingers on
Harp strings chiming time.
It could go wrong. Freedom means
Just that. So music moves us.


What was once merely
Freedom turns historical,
And into meaning.
Sometimes we glimpse both at once.
Why that red dress, that meadow?


These textures, these tones,
Now signify the decade
That gave birth to me.
We can wave our arms thus; we
Can make cool trailbacks. Discuss.


Time to sleep. I see
The kitchen window frames whirls
And capers of snow.
Immeasurable heaven
Of colliding galaxies.

# FEBRUARY
*(2020)*

**1st February (Saturday)**

We're all connected.
It's meant to be uplifting.
Then comes the virus.
Trade coming out of China.
Lies that will spread forever.


Are letters defunct?
From one soul to another,
Just the two of us.
Now, not you and I, but they,
Cannibalising all things.


If so, literature,
Such intimacy its blood,
Will go the same way.
There'll be only spectacle
And the correct opinions.

Around the station
An avenue of bare trees,
Asymmetrical.
Already spring paints the sky
And stirs a germ in old bones.


## 2<sup>nd</sup> February (Sunday)

Death may surprise us.
Daily life is nothing else
But senseless struggle.
What do I feel loyal to?
Some namelessness beyond this.


Three years a child star.
Television. Radio.
At eighteen she died
When a lorry driver sneezed.
Where have you gone, Charlotte Long?


An eternal spring.
On the edge of adventure.
How green it all was!

My nerves dew-drenched with strangeness.
Charlotte, I, too, might have lived.


Death only as close
As always, although chances
To dodge it decrease.
Why, then, bend to the future?
Why make my exit so stooped?


As the lotus bud
Cracks open, reveals the gold
In the crown of white,
Will the promise be fulfilled?
Will someday ever be now?


How is it these dreams
Of things that never can be,
Seem sometimes greater
Than all the known world of is?
Do others feel the same pull?


So easily lost.
Whatever is most alive.
Do you remember?
How can God be less than that?
Then, don't follow the lesser.

The ruined chapel
In the woods. The cobwebbed gate
Ajar. Memory.
But what is it that once lived?
What is it that was promised?

## 3rd February (Monday)

Mornings full of dread,
A raw day ahead of me,
Steering life alone.
Then, when evening comes at last,
Dread, too, since morning follows.


What do I fear most?
People, with all their demands
And all their judgements.
Yet, without them I would starve.
Rather, that's why I fear them.


This citalopram,
A weight tied to my ankle,
Pulling me under.

If only I could go down
To the bottom and stay there.


Why does it matter
How I feel as species die?
What does 'matter' mean?
It all seems unstoppable.
At least I don't have children.


These heroes on show,
Though most of us spend nights in,
Self-medicating.
"Your best isn't good enough."
Who cares? Just give us comfort.


How to conquer time?
Not while you still live, my friend;
Not when you are dead.
Even these novels, tangling
Setting and mind, are time-bound.


Our lived Atlantis—
Something of it yet remains.
Grey-day net curtains.
Let me occupy this nest
Of pooling wax like a flame.

Up the rusty steps
To the flat roof and the nook
By miracle mine.
Anyway, my tenancy.
Out of the rain, to sip tea.


### 4<sup>th</sup> February (Tuesday)

The boy, aspiring,
In success or in failure
Effaced by the man.
Or her, life's threshold death's frame,
As unreachable as him.


It was the eighties.
The world was reinvented.
Pop-up. Cleverer.
Still English summers were cool
And we played synths in Sherwood.


Conjunctions in time
Make experience unique.

I was fresh-faced then,
When New Romantics postured.
I wore green fluorescent socks.


## 5th February (Wednesday)

The tapestry stirs
In my mind's prehensile breeze,
Windchiming symbols.
New York—main streets and side streets;
A page of Japanese script.


Juxtapositions
Of symbols I understand
Summon a genie.
I, too, will bottle genies.
The world is alive with them.


Why did she choose me,
This muse half fairy half ghost?
I am unworthy.
Or did she want a cuckold
To watch and record her loves?

But who is art for?
The worthy, upright and whole?
If for them, not from.
So I negate, a eunuch
For the Fairy Kingdom's sake.


Roseate and blue,
The whole evening sky unreal.
Beneath it, the town.
Always to be with that sky,
No word of it from my mouth!


## 6<sup>th</sup> February (Thursday)

Rinsing the teapot,
I saw frost on roofs of cars
And was glad at it.
Yesterday I had complained
That the winter was too mild.


Is it that people
Are disagreeable, or

Is it that I am?
Either way, I need routine
To sustain my solitude.


Sunlight touched with frost.
On a day like this let me
Lean on the handrail
Of a footbridge over tracks
At a little train station.


February tree,
Against waking-trance pale blue,
Its bark silver-grey,
Barbed with buds like spearheads,
A fishing net for the moon.


Inspecting my plants,
Working on that long essay,
Writing more e-mails,
General business of the day.
But is there a safety net?

### 7ᵗʰ February (Friday)


Just to be at home.
Rattle the cutlery drawer,
Prepare my breakfast.
If there were no time limit,
Just to be at home would do.


It's not enough now,
This slow-motion suicide
As self-expression.
Decadent and unaware,
Your culture's walls protect you.


In the hinterland
Of an old, old destiny,
My ramshackle shack.
I still faintly remember
How I was turned from the path.


### 8ᵗʰ February (Saturday)


Is decline one-way,
As and since Nietzsche foresaw,

For the Western world?
With teachers fallen so low
How can their students now rise?


From the sixties on
Geek is as high as it gets.
Catchphrases, giggles,
Autopilot irony—
A world without memory.


For justice, for hope,
We support enlightened ads
From HSBC,
Burger King, Nike, Gillette.
We're the most enlightened yet.


A cheap and mobile
Workforce without family
Or national ties,
Isolated consumers—
Behold, our utopia!


Aging to the sound
Of traffic passing outside,
Like packed centuries.

One day I'll forget myself.
Strange, bitter-sweet signature.


### 9th February (Sunday)

Rain on the window
Shivers the lamp-post and trees
Into grey scribbles.
This flat's a chimney corner
Where wind whistles and shudders.


Somehow audible,
Bounced over five thousand miles,
The voice of a friend.
Final destinations blind,
We lift a hatch between lives.


Streetlights, on and on.
Memories. We had to sleep
In the cold parked car.
Before the world's edge appeared
All such things were wonderful.

The B11.
I rumble towards Thamesmead.
World of wet pavements.
The night, the lights and the rain.
Housing estates, flooding drains.


## 10th February (Monday)


The cold city lights—
How they used to frighten me.
High-rise density.
"You are here" is "You are lost."
Strangers colonise the sky.


Somewhere. Anywhere.
I've been blown from place to place.
Or sometimes I flew.
I don't think I can attend
Each funeral of each friend.


Yes, I have travelled.
A bus on a mountain road.
No one who knows me
Knowing where I was, thinking,
"It's enough." Another bend.

Getting my sea legs,
Living with history's roll.
The sad, ugly streets,
The bedlam of tweets, will pass.
I'll retire to my cabin.


## 11<sup>th</sup> February (Tuesday)

A childhood penfriend.
A show discovered by chance.
A lost B-side song.
There was another life once.
There's no trace of it today.


A strange semi-fame.
Convolvulus profusion,
But who notices?
Some are weeds in fame's garden.
As for me, I'm fond of weeds.


Nineteen eighty-two.
*Schoolgirl Chums* and *Dear Heart*.

I was ten years old.
The tender green of new leaves,
Sensitive to novelty.


Easily impressed?
In hindsight, the show was weak.
And yet I was touched.
All the heart-sweetness was in
Sketching new styles of dream.


These treasures long prized,
The mountain where I found them
Was a rubbish heap.
It's strange to look back and know
My sacred site was so low.


Still I can't believe
These fond trinkets are worthless.
Hold them to the light.
How richly they opalesce.
Is this Quixote's madness?

## 12<sup>th</sup> February (Wednesday)

Compared to past years
These poems come much harder,
All outside the zone.
Is it the citalopram?
I cling to a sheer cliff face.


Between not caring
And crushing anxiety,
Is there a sweet spot?
Overwhelmed and not caring
Are the same: I just lie down.


Seven Day Chemist,
Oh yeah, Seven Day Chemist!
Eight to eleven.
How pleasant to present there
My repeat prescription, yeah.


Deadlines and duties,
But if you don't bother me,
I won't bother you.
Let's go as slow as we can;
The whole world may blow over.

I'm worried about
My washing machine. "20",
On my T-shirt, blurs,
Disappears, as the spin goes
Faster, clears the atmosphere.


Guilty! I'm effete.
I admit the charge. We're all,
Anyway, sentenced
To death. Will I weep beneath
The guillotine? Why not? Yes.


The end of the world
Will expose me, finally,
To myself. How cruel!
May the wall between myself
And me not easily fall.


In the school grounds stands
The werewolf tree, jagged, bent,
Bristling with twigs.
From this tree, someday, a tale
Will come, please God, ere I'm spent.

### 13th February (Thursday)

Rain on the window.
Gentle clusters of tapping,
As if to say, "Rest."
Such are the voices I would
Magnify—the real Sky News.


The phrase 'surf the web'
These days I find apposite.
The wave is cubist.
Ever breaking, life and death;
Some are breaking, some broken.


### 14th February (Friday)

"In twenty years' time."
When someone speaks those words now,
They echo against
The wall at my life-span's end.
I can only move forward.

I've wasted more time
Already than I have left.
Can I use despair
And hope to change not chain me?
Can I become serious?


If I can't become
Serious, why not just live
Like a fool? Do I
Think I won't be up to death?
But fools die, too, every day.


Waiting in my cell,
I'm not ready for the end.
But even waiting
Effects a change. The process
Is perfect. I've had enough.


## 15<sup>th</sup> February (Saturday)

In search of lost time.
Proust was dying as he wrote,
As all who write are.
Somehow in that final book
Lost time, at last, was regained.

"Someday you'll read Proust,"
He said. "When the time is right."
And I believed him.
There in that Soho café,
Time claimed our conversation.


Not so much bitter,
These days more puzzled, perplexed.
Is this who I am?
Strange to be so limited,
Twisted into singlehood.


You hear a new song
And seem to understand it.
What is its message?
That such songs are possible.
Your understanding proves it.


After death, what then?
Such total uncertainty
Frames all human life.
Yet I'm here chopping mushrooms.
This must be an adventure.

## 16th February (Sunday)

We awake to this—
Something in particular,
Sometimes something new.
We become hip to space-time,
As if we already knew.


Life engenders life.
Tom Baker's voice windborne like
Dandelion seeds.
Who, then, demands that we live
In fear? What are their motives?


I, too, have my fears:
Surveillance, gene-editing,
The whole sick mixture
Of sneering triumph, self-hate
And unctuousness beneath.

## 17$^{th}$ February (Monday)

It's really caught on,
Predicting the ends of things.
Why do we do it?
To make others unhappy?
"There's no hope. Despair, like me!"


No one could invent
This tea-and-biscuits England,
Both dry and twinkling.
Sublime triviality
Set in dark infinity.


So the dilemma:
To live in complacency
Or helpless terror.
Either way, the same end comes.
Procreation is faith's leap.


Keep painting, painting.
Like a silkworm eating leaves
And excreting silk.
Fill as much of the canvas
As you can before you die.

Days are all we have.
Pebbles on the window sill
In the seat of now.
But unlike the stones, we're moved,
And our days are countable.


## 18th February (Tuesday)

From lack of guidance
How many lives are wasted?
All that is required
Is that the wise should become
Organised. There are no wise.


Our brains peak, I've read,
In our forties. If only
Things had been explained
When I was at school. But I
Was led by cultureless fools.

Instead I must trust
There was a reason that I
Wandered such by-ways.
That I might learn from regret?
Serve as a bad example?


I go for a walk
Partly so that I'll feel warm
When I come back in.
If skylines were not deadlines,
Life might always be this sweet.


## 19th February (Wednesday)


A weak scavenger,
Sheltering in dank ruins,
I, too, have a world.
Weeds illuminate the rocks.
I hymn them in rotting books.


This hermit creature
Has noticed something funny
He keeps to himself.
If not for people he'd know
Nothing at all of God's wrath.

Three score years and ten,
Of which two score years and ten
Will not come again.
At least suicide now seems
Redundant. It's fine—I'll wait.


You have a secret,
You must but cannot keep it,
Like a mounting sneeze.
Don't dig a hole and whisper—
Write a book! There's no echo.


Days—one to each dog.
Does this mean one of his own?
To keep? Not on loan?
I'd like to know who said so.
Did they know something I don't?


Days are sky and sun,
Which share roots with the divine.
You're standing in one.
Or you could be lying down,
Or coming round to see me.

Like a long drum roll—
Faster, faster, dizzier,
Until the last beat.
Is that how the deaths will be?
And then—what curtain rises?


## 20th February (Thursday)

Decreasing jobs, skills,
Agency—self-driving cars.
Humans never saw
A genie in a bottle
They didn't want to let out.


Seven billion.
All thinking the world is theirs
And all horrified
At the mess. It's surprising
That we're organised at all.


Around five o'clock
At this time of year, the sun,
With gold post-rain glow,

Burns pale in the net curtains
In transfiguring decline.


### 21st February (Friday)


The constant subtext—
People like me should shut up,
Find somewhere to die.
Still I'm expected to cry
When the licence fee is scrapped.


There's always someone
We're allowed—*compelled*—to hate.
These days it's 'gammon'.
Or those others we must not
Mention. At least it's progress.


Are the stars moving?
No, it's insect-clouds of planes,
Crunchy dragonflies.
Sparks over the winter park—
Is it these who preach to me?

This old fantasy
Has only led me astray.
I remain loyal.
After all, what else is there?
The world, itself, is nothing.


### 22<sup>nd</sup> February (Saturday)

Since the vote to leave
I've noticed a sharp increase
In online outbursts
Of gerontophobia.
Guess what! Pete Townshend grew old.


Literally a tweet:
"We need immigrants to do
The work that we don't
Want to." This is the moral
High ground. Lily Allen Land.


Have I been doing
Mortality maths (a phrase
Coined by Paphides)?

Larkin wrote about it, too.
I refer to 'Reference Back'.


So many people
Whose plans for the world entail
That my crops must fail.
The world's a game of pinball.
My dreams fall back down the hole.


Just don't expect me
To cheer for your side, that's all.
Sophie A. Lewis,
Charting the end goal, provides
Sufficient *reductio*.


### 23<sup>rd</sup> February (Sunday)

Sacred history.
The Word is like a fountain,
In each now reborn.
We cannot understand it.
It joins us in love and war.

On the edge of sleep,
My mind is whisked in the air,
Like foam as waves crash.
All that once seemed obvious
Just melts. Mere habits of thought.


## 24<sup>th</sup> February (Monday)

It's something I call
The Pacifist's Dilemma.
How can your ideal
Scale up? Say 'we' and you strip
Others of their self-defence.


Is the world ending
Or is it the internet
That makes me think so?
"Take sides!" they scream. Whoever
Wins, a new extreme begins.


Who would follow us?
Our charity has become
Complex self-loathing,
Forming a recursive loop.
No way back, no way forward.

I'm only sickened
By the things people wish for.
To merge with machines?
After everything we know
Of Zuckerberg? That's the dream?


Dark bellies of clouds
Tinged orangey-pink as if
Beyond the skyline
A great furnace was dying.
Cold air. I'm almost ready.


The leafless poplars,
Or I think that's what they are,
Tall and feather-shaped,
By the side of the footpath,
None but they know my longing.


### 25th February (Tuesday)


As often happens,
The same product in slightly
Different packaging.
Paracetamol, sixteen
Caplets. Music. Countries. Lives.

Before we begin,
I feel myself caving in.
How can I presume?
Later, I reconsider.
Why don't I take my own side?


Just outside, someone
Had tossed or dropped a bottle
Of something called 'Yop'.
What a disgusting object.
I didn't want to touch it.


Behind the poplars,
A rainbow gathering strength,
Spanning the valley.
At the opposite skyline,
Rain clouds yellow-gold with haze.


If I ever find
A house all agree is mine,
I'll call it Eden.
There'll be a grove of holly,
Crows to caw at dawn's window.

## 26th February (Wednesday)


No central heating.
Going in I wondered how
I'd get through winter.
Now, in my blanket poncho,
Sun glows behind my eyelids.


Carefree in the rain,
I could be fifteen, or eight.
Why not start again?
Despite my grey hairs, somewhere,
In a box, lies unused youth.


I can't help thinking
My slippers are *très* modern.
Memory-foam soles
Shape themselves to your feet and
Within days fall to pieces.


I don't assume that
Others think the same as me.
They tell me what they
Think, so I know they don't—tell
Me, assuming I'll agree.

### 27<sup>th</sup> February (Thursday)

Ilfracombe summers.
Led Zeppelin kept me hopeful.
Young legs in tight jeans.
A kiosk selling lollies
Would give me daydream gooseflesh.


I drew the curtains—
Reassuring morning rain.
That was eight o'clock.
Before ten, an itchy glance—
When did the rain change to snow?


Against the sunset
The blackness of the branches
Is like ink still wet.
Late winter/early spring brings
Strange, sweet, limpid growing pains.


Train to Charing Cross.
Facing backward I see pass
Offices, billboard.

Suddenly a rose window,
Unreachable among bricks.


This morning brief snow.
This evening cherry blossom
At Blackheath Station.
I change trains here in the cold,
Heading home from the opera.


What is it you see
When you know someone's angry?
Is it seen, or felt?
Sometimes you even hear it.
Seen, felt, heard, the same something.


### 28<sup>th</sup> February (Friday)

The satisfaction—
Just to come back to a place
Of my own, although
Interaction is something
I can't escape forever.

In the end, I can't
Undo who I am and start
Again. I always
Feel strange pretending, though, yes,
Consensus comes with violence.


I made the mistake
(Et cetera) of reading
Reviews of *Carmen*.
"Toxic masculinity."
So, all our thinking's been done.


Paintings of Saint George
Are alive for me once more.
I can hear the saint
Crying, "Die, die, die, die, DIE!"
I won't say who he's slaying.


Where once I was ranked
With the right-on punkular,
Now I might be deemed
A shade avuncularer.
Might I go two shades far'er?

Nothing is more real
Than the sound of tyres in rain.
Meaningless? Mundane?
No. To me it's cosmic. 'Real'
Should not imply 'meaningless'.


## 29<sup>th</sup> February (Saturday)

I started unsure.
Now I don't want to come off
These apathy pills.
I'm afraid to care again.
In the end I'm still afraid.


I've said this before:
If you want a snail to race,
Don't prod. Spurs don't work.
Like snails I'm mostly slow, but
Quick to shrink back in my shell.


The jokes, so you know
They're informal, subversive,
Contain shibboleths.
Fail to laugh and it's noted.
Soon you learn what 'outside' means.

When was I last here
Round Highbury and Islington?
Years pass, I'm still me.
The same loneliness for all,
But this is mine, and won't last.


The darkness so dark,
Streetlights, station lights, look like
Loneliness itself.
My dry eyes sting with tiredness.
My end is a question mark.

# MARCH
*(2021)*

## 1<sup>st</sup> March (Monday)

Staring at train tracks.
Was I really serious?
Well, no one will know.
Yes, now I'm dappled with blame
Because, alone, I've survived.


Strange to be othered.
Have I really lost a friend
Because of my mind?
Where can I spend this anger?
My voice, a card that's declined.


And altruism—
Is this a one-way demand,
Taxing the poorest?
Well, I can't pay, so let me
Stay away from politics.

You hate them—don't you?—
Ultimately—the people.
Some of them, at least.
Including me, by the way—
They who refuse to be saved.


Amid litter, masks.
The sky is a great, grey lid.
The chill has returned.
"Can't you see what's happening?"
Words made suspect in advance.


### 2nd March (Tuesday)


Glitter-swarm starfish
Devour the pullulating
Corpse of a seal pup.
Ocean worms cry from its eyes.
Glamorous and abandoned.


A song in my head.
What's it doing there? 'Field Work'
By Thomas Dolby.

There's something I've yet to do.
A call to reawaken.


Interrogation
In a university
In America.
He tries to say he's not white;
He's Jewish. "That's spicy white!"


### 3rd March (Wednesday)


Slowly to advance
Like a coach drawn by horses,
Through cloud-sheltered days.
Before the morning basin
As if packing the day's case.


Those promising days
Were the thing they promised, then
This strange present came.
You can't lay your hand on Kate
As she was. She can't, either.

Why always this choice:
Whether to ignore, submit,
Sidestep or confront?
Assumptions as if designed
To round up the dissenters.


You receive from them
The virtues by which you judge
The ones who bequeath.
But it's worse than that. Often
The heirloom is mistreated.


The question transforms
The questioner. The question!
Not yet the answer.
The initiate surprised
By the sudden, "What is mind?"


Evenings are paler.
The arc of days makes a yawn.
No wonder buds stretch.
I haven't yet been noticed.
Maybe that's why I'm still free.

## 4th March (Thursday)


With age it grows clear
That you only have one life,
Most of it now had.
You must strategise and yet
Forget death to start afresh.


Biases emerge
In my selection of things
When getting things done.
Sand accumulates into
A dune; shifts or collapses.


Strangely degrading,
Though everyone now does it,
This online dating.
Even 'meat markets', so-called,
First served other purposes.


A debutante at
A dance could be flaunted by
Solicitous aunts
Without the least cost to her
Innocence. Or am I dense?

Briar Rose, dormant.
Even while asleep, I've aged.
Handsome princes pass
To where the thorns are less thick,
And the blossom is fresher.


## 5<sup>th</sup> March (Friday)

The weekend won't stay.
No sooner here than it's packed,
Tired of us, moves on.
So our lives are gathered up
In glib sections, then cast off.


Jauntily alone . . .
Must I disclose each moment
To the public mind?
Anyhow, hands in pockets,
In long coat and hat—how free!


Apropos nicknames,
You should never choose your own—
It gives you away.

Sartre's journal: *Modern Times*.
Toads inflate themselves just so.


The moderns? Perverts.
Always seeking some excuse
To empty bladders.
"Man's nature is incomplete!"
Then comes the jet in your eyes.


But the church—come on,
Let's not shilly-shally—chose
Her own nickname, too.
Others could only react.
And see! Look where that's got us.


Montaigne proposes
Socrates as a model,
But our heroes now?
We've stared at clay feet so long
We can't even raise our heads.


Hashtag readtheroom.
Funny how such words take on
Their own tone of voice.
I hear: "Our room is better
Than anyone who enters."

## 6ᵗʰ March (Saturday)

Another one-day
Extension after the end—
Is that how I should
Think of it? Surplus? So then,
Should I spend it whimsically?


Childless. To decide
If this decision was mine
Might be beyond me.
Either way, it's setting fast,
Irreversible default.


Footnotes to Plato—
That's philosophy. Footnotes
To my own failure—
That's me. Strange to prance in dust
And wind thus redundantly.


I can take the cold
Today. I can take the cold
Tomorrow, but when

I think of these six months spent
Shivering, I almost crack.


Magnetic tension.
I must resist ideas
We attribute to
Conspiracy theorists.
But then, that begs the question.


Lockdown forever.
People forever snarling,
"Stay the fuck at home!"
Bezos crowned king of the world.
And you understand it all.


You understand it,
So everyone else should, too.
But understand what?
"To question is to deny.
Don't make that mistake again."


Gaslighting? I write
By gaslight. Gaslit, I see
My twisted shadow
On the page. This way, that way—
By your light, it's all insane.

## 7th March (Sunday)

That others exist—
This is a reproach to me.
Why am I not they?
But they don't seem to notice,
They cancel each other out.


"If you wear a mask
You're a twat." "If you don't wear
A mask you're a twat."
I somehow believe both sides.
What kind of creature am I?


"These people are cunts."
"We're all of us flawed beings."
Which way do I turn?
One way is pious pretence;
The other, false reduction.


There comes a time when
You can't talk anymore. Then

You must kill, kill, kill.
That time is approaching fast.
We're agreed on that, at least.


Clouds themselves like hills
Just protruding from sky-mist,
Tints dusk-blue and peach.
No wonder some flee the world,
By which we mean 'flee people'.


Terraced cooking smells.
Figures lit in upstairs rooms.
Kids dash from a shop.
Let your pulse grow quieter.
The dream train crosses the bridge.


### 8th March (Monday)


They think they're claiming
The world as their own. Give it
Twenty years, at most.
They've just set the precedent
To be dispossessed in turn.

I was born into
A world now disappearing.
They cheer its decline.
That much I must bear. But they
Insist that I cheer with them.


Empowerment is
The process of revealing
That corruption is
A human universal.
Yes, we should all have a turn.


I smile a strange smile.
What kind of world would it be
That met their wishes?
Would I shrivel like a witch
In their caring circle-jerk?


With each new person
I meet, I know I must hide
Who I am, while they
Smile safely, forever right.
I'd like to tear their throats out.

But venting aside,
How strange to see these faces,
Knowing they assume
That I'm like them. This divide—
And I'm on the other side.


Do I feel such rage,
Such sadness, when not exposed
To the internet?
Considerably less. Am I
So suggestible? Well, yes.


Literature was once
A closed confessional box.
With the internet,
The author doxed, it's become,
Instead, a struggle session.


We're just a branch of
Advertising. If only
There were a greeting
Like this: "I'm a piece of shit,
But so are you, so don't start."

It seems that I'm bound
For somebody else's hell.
The question is: whose?
I can't believe all the things
You severally want me to.


**9th March (Tuesday)**


Mary Carmichael,
Writing one hundred years gone,
Had no need of hate.
Men no longer held her down.
What of life's adventure now?


A patch of shadow,
Where a wall dams the sun, mints
This contrast: shade, light.
So today is fresh and warm,
Displacing a block of cold.


White cherry blossoms.
Not the first I've seen this year,
And not the whole tree.

How many more times will spring
Hang its cape on my coathook?

## 10th March (Wednesday)

This reinforcement
Of the fear of death, as if
I am consciousness.
But this wave that takes me in
Is older, will last longer.


Without me, I fear,
These back-of-hand things will go
Unnoticed, be lost.
Just to reassure myself,
I play that old song again.


The blocked-up chimney
Still shudders with wind. This flat—
The rain's music box.
There's no especial story,
Just life's seashell at my ear.

A narrow entrance
Into a low stone passage
Like a mountain cave.
If I could only squeeze through,
Would I cross into the sky?


**11<sup>th</sup> March (Thursday)**


For instance, no one
Can continue my reading;
They didn't start it.
This corner of consciousness
Collapsed, its shelves will empty.


Is the worry this?:
Multiculturalism means
World monoculture,
And likewise, theosophy,
Homogenised religion.


Terribly more-ish.
Differences are just in tastes.
Dipping Doritos

In the salsa or sour cream
Of hate. Everyone does it.


## 12<sup>th</sup> March (Friday)

Postpone the battle!
The wind is a lullaby
And the skies are grey.
Take up embroidery, sit
By the window. War rolls on.


The obvious joke:
Will Scots nationalists who hate
England now be charged?
Hate crime, eh? You fools. You swines.
Now try to legislate love.


"No one's saying that."
Really? Let me show you, then,
Today's Twitter feed,
Where your side say anything
And no one changes their mind.

## 13<sup>th</sup> March (Saturday)

A basic setting:
I feel myself surrounded
By hostile forces.
I withdraw before the thrusts
Of their pelvic self-belief.


We're all male. Let me
Explain why. We mostly keep
Our elytra closed.
We must hide our light because
Flashing threatens everyone.


The core of being,
The naked self, the life-force,
Must be kept holstered.
Draw and the whole world is tense
In a Mexican stand-off.


But there are parades
Where similar private parts
Are safely displayed.
If you don't find one to join,
How ashamed you feel, alone.

The rawness I feel,
The magnetic repulsion,
Cannot be escaped.
It's me. How strange to confess—
Yes, it's weird, but this is me.


I find myself here.
Although I've never left me,
It's still a surprise.
From this and that, I've diverged;
Now I'm a theist, and worse.


They come. They smash through
Barriers. They break windows.
Mob pedestrians.
American violence sets
The Western world's agenda.


The firewall's down.
The spies are here in your home.
Just turn yourself in.
All undesirables—we
Know who you are. We're coming.

Humans—fair play—are
Enterprisingly stupid.
Always some new thing.
Always surprising. Only
Caring when their tricks backfire.


## 14th March (Sunday)


The proclamation
Of seventeen sixty-three
Was flouted. Since then
There have reigned perversity,
Destruction, democracy.


Like foxes stealing
Chickens, they know no shame. Yet
They use shame against
Those who question or dissent.
Why am I so defenceless?


The speed with which they
Switch leaves me breathless, sick. First
They stigmatise those

Protesting lockdown, then wail
When they are policed in turn.


Moving zone to zone.
Here, they police your sadness;
There, your happiness.
Here, sex; there, lack of sex. Walls
Pulled down are built back higher.


If there were someone
Who was right, *simpliciter*,
Then the rest of us
(Because it's not me) would die,
Swallowed by that omni-sun.


Our sharing in Is
Makes of each I a world-hub.
If two should collide
It's universicide, risked
Both by speech and by silence.


We're expected to
Know everything. But I know
Nothing. Then again,
It's dangerous not to judge,
But I've no time for research.

## 15th March (Monday)


Death is near again.
Some books will fall out of print.
I am sick with dread.
Back to zero, but older,
And each true word brings chaos.


Boundaries are so
Important, they say, and then
They violate yours.
Pillagers scream for their rights,
And I'm a public throughway.


Those I can talk to
Grow fewer. I blame myself,
But what can I do?
I cannot think what I don't.
I am a flux of self-doubt.


Hate crime. Everyone
Is guilty of a hate crime.
But who defines it?

Let's just hope they frame it right,
To snare those we hate, not us.


What am I? Something
So terrible that it must
Edge through unnoticed.
From birth right up until death,
Without that confrontation.


Their good; my evil.
They pursue their truth; it's like
Watching spiders mate.
They're inspired by vicious thoughts,
Raise children, claim their future.


All that's asked of us
Is the impossible. Look:
First John, 3:15.
We've hardly known light at all.
Can we live without darkness?


The young manspread with
Their opinions. They don't know
They're setting the tone.
On the one hand they push, but
They don't expect resistance.

So tired. Unvaried
Failure. Lack of money, plus
This loss of belief.
I'm finally persuaded
That I should be slow-faded.

## 16<sup>th</sup> March (Tuesday)

Why does a lost game
Continue? Mine or the world's.
I've tried to shake off
What I have become, but my
Own life overpowers me.


Minds meet, but some minds
Repel me. But what is it
I smell? That these are
People whose mistakes are not
Of the heart, but of the will.

## 17<sup>th</sup> March (Wednesday)

We've spoken enough
Of these things, though we'll return
To them all too soon.
Without the Silver Key, none
Of this deserves the least glance.


My age is such that
Earthly affairs exhaust me,
But what else is there?
Without dreams, all is unreal,
But lived or unlived, dreams fade.


In 'The Silver Key'
Lovecraft speaks of Dream almost
Apophatically.
It is not the occult, not
Religion, not irony.


So the box that holds
The Silver Key is carved with
Shuddersome demons.
Turn back. Do not open. This
Has no known imprimatur.

## 18th March (Thursday)


Nature boy, hating
The old faith, going back to
What he supposes
Is the older, referring
The world always to the world.


"Hey, just be yourself!"
But mine's in conflict with yours.
You haven't noticed,
Because I've effaced myself
For your sake. Have you, for mine?


The skies, recently!
Let me at least have the skies.
Clouds gilled like a shark.
Such beautiful grey darkness.
And here, a blackthorn's white spray.


Without transcendence,
They're like children at the stage

Of toilet humour:
Ploppy rebels with farty
Marxism, flaunting bogeys.


Nightmare, I think, is
Contraction. It is smaller
Than reality.
A sealed immanence, what we
Might call 'ideology'.


My fear, then, is
That someone's nightmare will be
Made obligatory.
We must be allowed to seek
That larger reality.


That figure again—
Ten years until the world ends,
Whatever 'world' means,
But you've made existence hell.
Tell me, why shouldn't I cheer?

## 19ᵗʰ March (Friday)

Trapped into living.
I must force myself to care.
Who is this helping?
There's sunlight on the carpet,
But eviction always looms.


Earthquake nausea.
The feeling of no fixed ground,
Nothing beyond doubt.
People are tribal? Of course.
Question and you'll lose your home.


During the exam
There comes a point when you know
How badly you've done.
There's no recovering. Still
The clock's minute hand keeps time.


Above me, branches—
An umbrella of chaos
With no canopy.
Through twisted ribs, the new moon;
Through this madness, I, alone.

## 20<sup>th</sup> March (Saturday)

In 'The Silver Key'
The Bohemian set is
Quite familiar:
An inconsistent mix of
Hedonists, Nietzscheans, prigs.


The first census. When
I heard of it, how evil
It seemed. Another
Contraction, vacuum-packing
Humanity as the known.


Now, a dilemma.
The more different tribes there are,
The more violence. Yes,
The state is an achievement,
But whose this monopoly?

The first person. Such
Time-and-place sights, such strange blooms,
Such networks of thought!
Can it be this is wasted
On a coward such as me?


I think I've got it.
The problem with the Stoics:
For them, suspension
Was enough. You're dead, or not,
Knowledge restricted to life.


### 21st March (Sunday)


"You will own nothing
And you will be happy." Threats?
Promises? Commands?
But happiness cannot be
Promised. Not promises, then.


They ask, no, tell us,
To ignore the universe.
Outer and inner.
I've struggled my whole life, but
Still I cannot obey them.

Indestructible
Nodes of infinity burn
And burn forever.
That's what Hell means. Eternal
Contradiction in God's heart.


What madness is this?
You grovel before your own
Reversed mirror-self.
"We have failed. Rule over us!
Destroy us! We deserve it."


The overlords you
Welcome were gestated in
The human matrix.
Group self-hatred imposed by
Those above on those below.


I use the word 'heart'
Meaningfully. Imagine
Not being able.
But you're fresh from their table,
Your smile a stitched scalpel scar.

The beast. A heart pounds
In the grim recesses of
This meat processor.
The Beast of Chaos tamed. Hail!
Salute the Beast of Order.


## 22<sup>nd</sup> March (Monday)

In Tanzania,
The bank notes, staying so long
In circulation,
Were grim, shrivelled rags. Better
Dirty money than cashless.


In the restaurant,
Well, someone's house, he was asked
To choose a chicken.
Slaughtered and served, there and then.
What we eat here—it's not meat.


Money honed into
Abstraction, a light-sabre
Of sorcery for

Lawyers in warring factions,
The losers, slaves to blackmail.


I'm behind a bar.
Whoever hired me left no
Instructions. People
Crowd round, shout orders. I can't
Keep up. No one relieves me.


## 23<sup>rd</sup> March (Tuesday)

I just am alone.
Where I go the vacuum goes.
What I want's wanting.
There's simply no such thing as
A relationship with me.


We flail, caught between
Torpor and panic, helpless
Because divided.
The trap was laid long ago.
At least, I can believe it.

I can be unmade?
Well, what's so bad about that?
Life has unmade me.
To unmake my unmaking
Might even be to make me.


Those hooves clop again,
So clear on the hushed tarmac,
They stir the day's veil.
Black-plumed horses draw a hearse,
Passing in ominous peace.


### 24th March (Wednesday)


As if life's flirting
With a flash of underskirts—
Pink cherry blossoms.
Your heart swoons to the unreal.
Life mocks you: "Make the first move."


Make your move quickly.
In a few weeks, blossoms fall.

You can still enjoy
The long summer, true. Winter
Will make known how wise your grab.


I grabbed nothing. Life
Said: "Be a hero, or be
A rogue." Too slow, I
Became a mere voyeur of
Trees and seasons—a poet.


They gave. They pushed from
The back of the boat in which
The human future
Was nested. I look back now
And see them, tired, receding.


Tittling the top
Of the partially blooming
Blackthorn tree, tiny,
Dotty birds. They hop. Feathers
Flicker. Little trills. Flit off.

### 25th March (Thursday)


When was the last time
You saw there thrilling, the stars?
The stars. Remember?
No one talks about them now.
Were they real? The stars. Who knows?


Thinking of Folkestone.
Outside the station entrance,
The summer stretches.
When you're young, you wait there, your
Expectation not yet slack.


People I'll never
See again—Keiko, for one,
From Kumamoto.
A uniqueness arises,
Then it's gone. Such untold ghosts.


Zugzwang on the scale
Of the human race. It's here.
The Saviour Machine.
Human nature meant it was
Always waiting—our nightmare.

Across the moon, clouds,
Like a membranous process
Of non-human dream.
Just keep the silver light clean.
Give me those clouds for pillows.


Who can I talk to
In the sublunary world?
How filthy they are.
They'd think I'm mad. All that's left
Is the moonlight and my mind.


Is this how it feels
To be tricked and tormented
By Descartes' demon?
I can't tell if they want me
To be frightened or carefree.


### 26<sup>th</sup> March (Friday)

Sleep-walking, they say.
No, it's sleep paralysis,
This technocracy.
A digital hag rides us,
And we might never awake.

Contagious feelings,
Contagious thoughts. Are they mine?
Is that question mine?
Someone, somewhere, had a plan
To demoralise. It worked.


To keep informed, or
Keep misinformed: which is it?
A donkey is trapped
Between two piles of data,
Sceptically starving to death.


The West spawned the Left.
Maybe we deserve to fall.
Such strange emotions.
Our best has become our worst,
So we hand China what's hers.


Just rearguard action.
I know I'm leaving the world.
I know it's not mine.
As long as the would-be meek
Don't catch up with me, it's fine.

## 27<sup>th</sup> March (Saturday)

Like waiter training.
Everyone goes through it. Don't
Take it personally.
It's just a routine, they say.
But the horror when you snap!


Satan makes you hate
Yourself; Lucifer makes you
Proud. What lies between?
"A distant star called Home." But
Human voices are marsh lights.


Twixt Heaven and Earth—
Socrates, question made flesh,
Stinging the polis.
Even he cleaved to home, chose
Hemlock, and honoured the gods.


Not just flat answers,
But the slow-solving tides of
Unplumbed duration.
Many errors collage this
Syrupy river of truth.

Cherry trees at night.
A special fragility.
Perfection shivers.
Pink-white petals, naked, fall,
Litter in trickles of rain.


### 28th March (Sunday)

Can the Ultimate
Use the lived experience
(So-called) of my self?
Then why wouldn't it? If not,
Do the rights revert to me?


Why did consciousness
Snag on my nail, making me
As if everything?
Is it punishing itself?
Why live through an NPC?


Distinctly a slump.
Should I pause and go deeper,

Unearth recurrent
Causes? Or should I climb out,
Trudge on? Which will waste less time?


### 29<sup>th</sup> March (Monday)


A future in which
All non-vegans are reviled,
Their statues clawed down.
The analogy is not
Exact, but they never are.


Why are books wasted
On me? Because I'm childless?
Because I'm ignored?
No, because I'm a writer,
And not a person at all.


'Let your freak flag fly'
Means, 'Caricature yourself',
'Remake childhood's teams'.
You can't just be interested
In bees, no—"I'm a bee gurl!"

It's strange that we care
About being good at all,
Cannibals like us.
When I say this people think
I'm evil. True, but it hurts.


On cue, a kind of
Fluvial warmth in the air.
Officially spring.
There was a tree out there with
Buds at the end of each twig.


Why not love castles
When the Stelliferous age
Whizzes whimsically?
Why not read old romances,
Floppy and voluminous?


I felt I must sit,
Closed my eyes. A harmony
Of birds' mixed woodwind.
Sun on my tired face, soft air.
A blessèd change—sanity.

## 30th March (Tuesday)

Sunlight made crystal
In the small, frosted window,
As on frozen waves.
The soft freshness of morning,
Youth gently, briefly renewed.


To be established
Means to claim or tame something:
A horse, a spouse, land.
I've accumulated, yes—
Books at scattered addresses.


Marduk, Truth-Teller.
They invested him, kneeling,
With authority
Over them. What thing in me
Decides what's worthy of truth?


They pursue their truth
With interest, thus declare
Its value, their sense
Of the good. And what do they
Find Good? Sneering debasement.

The PayPal helpline.
Stuck in the time-crushing maze
Of a system bug.
When something works, her voice brims
With gladness. Time is redeemed.


"They laughed at Noah."
And maybe they'll laugh at you,
But you're not Noah.
Disasters will happen, but
Regardless of predictions.


Some kind of normal,
Some kind of real, is needed,
That's all, to make do,
To stop us questioning and
To make us question—a guide.


Seeing my life now
Contingent-made-actual,
Means seeing it more
In the third person. How strange
That he is me—forever.

## 31ˢᵗ March (Wednesday)

A writer's estate
Is a problem. Writers are
Frequently heirless.
Human attention's too scarce
To save much from death's air-raid.


Mere cat's paws of wind
On civilisation's lake,
And see what's stirred up!
Wailing, groaning, rolling eyes,
Dementing, they prophesy.


This particular
Thing must die. Not only that,
It must know its death.
So, this thing must have an I.
This particular thing. Me.

# APRIL
*(2022)*

## 1st April (Friday)

My thoughts, by habit,
Like anxious bacteria,
Breed in problem cracks.
This desk, for instance, now slopes,
Less than a year since purchase.


Why don't they settle
So readily on higher
Peaks? Sacramental
Snow refined from sun, vapour,
Air. Why do they creep so low?


All standards ruined.
Slow slippage sighs to a fall.
Skills, goods, services.
It's like one of those bad dreams
Where everything keeps breaking.

I awoke early.
The metal steps to this flat
Were like a gong struck.
I looked and saw no one there,
Just white ice on the flat roof.


A door thumps below.
The belly of a teacup
Feels hot in my hands.
While I watch, April Fool's snow
Flurries, then stops. And now sun.


Comfort's citadel
Besieged by Time's infantry.
Being lost, Time wins.
One problem down, more drive in.
The very nature of things.


Until yesterday,
For weeks, even months, I was
Bound in strange suspense.
Like something I don't quite get:
A problem is not a doom.

## 2nd April (Saturday)

That odd corner shop
Selling tobacco and toys.
Two quaintly cramped halves.
Walls treasure-dark with packed shelves:
Goodies whose source was unknown.


Eighties' Barnstaple.
Looking forward to magic,
I didn't know then
That I had it. Soon it went.
How shall we ever meet now?


It's true, mental fight
By itself is not enough,
But right now there's not
Enough mental fight. To build
Here a new Jerusalem.


England and childhood.
For me they are become one.
Both lie behind me.
Both make me what I am. Don't
Rob this child of belonging.

The apex problem?
No-objective-right-or-wrong
Times global-arms-race.
What do they have in common?
Something that we call 'science'.


First, the family,
The forgotten foundation.
Only from this seed
Grows transcendence of the seed.
So we cultivate the world.


### 3rd April (Sunday)


A certain degree
Of stability, even
With income so low.
I have no place in this world,
Yet here's my morning routine.


The state of nature—
If it was not Hobbesian
That's only because

The family is the word
Containing social meaning.


Without such a word,
How speak of fraternity?
'Speak of' meaning 'live'.
Always a compact kernel
Germinates and ramifies.


Perhaps, at the time,
You did not question whether,
How long, how often,
Had no thought of ever. Now
Years have elapsed. None come back.


Forging common sense,
Like diverting a river.
Forward's this way now.
The alternative trickle
Now a mandatory torrent.


So many changes,
And all of them common sense.
Haven't you noticed?
By definition, most choose
The numbers. Change, change again.

Only the will, blind
Will. *Sinister, dexter, next.*
Headless. Amorphous.
Each centipede segment grasps,
Degrades, crushes, still marches.


Only eighty years
Into the nuclear age.
Is the grass different?
Has nature shrunk, outmoded?
What are our season-words now?


### 4<sup>th</sup> April (Monday)

I light a candle.
A rainy Monday morning.
Ethan does dishes.
Sadly, the morning will wane;
The drab adventure resumes.


A whole day of this—
Of blankets, candles and rain—
That's what I wish for.

Of few words spoken, those low
And pleasant, tolling, "All's well!"


I crave still waters,
But time always runs, leaves us
Nothing but shallows.
Unless we find the day's deeps,
Just a succession of days.


What is the long view?
Are we to our descendants
As the Ancient Greeks
Or Han are to us? Do they
Care for us? Should we for them?


Climb, there is Heaven.
Dig, our roots are family.
Perhaps these two things.
From family: tribes, nations.
Lost without Heaven's Mandate.


A caterpillar
Shat upon me as I picked
It from the pavement.
Depositing it in some
Twigs of privet, I walked on.

### 5<sup>th</sup> April (Tuesday)

"It's a marathon."
Past halfway, I'm still going.
Aching, tired, steady.
There are so many of us,
Is anyone watching me?


With one problem solved,
I'm lifted on an updraft.
How high can I go?
Strange not knowing. Solo flight
Without aim or instruction.


Earth-scale problems, too.
The double nature of news:
Warnings defeat us.
Let us enjoy the updrafts;
We might even clear the clouds.


Acceleration,
Rousing motion, but towards

What destination?
Or is it a connection?
Will we be travelling on?


Say the end's certain.
I take up a paperback—
Still it involves me.
Story is eternity
In suspense. Always waiting.


### 6<sup>th</sup> April (Wednesday)

Rich, invisible
Tendons of meaning—feel them
In details at hand.
The world's body moves with these.
Why care for parts and not whole?


Another word for
Everything—the world. The from
And to of all we
Take and give, of all mad plans.
I leave you all that all leave.

Leaves of literature
Have steeped in my gut so long,
A strange tea ferments.
Almost ready to pour now.
Daigomi almost complete.


Gloomy afternoon.
I take a shower. Thunder
Summons harder rain.
A lad came round this morning;
The flush once more is working.


The horrible thing
Might happen. If we're helpless,
Why punish ourselves?
If we're hopeless we can't help
Ourselves. We might as well hope.


### 7<sup>th</sup> April (Thursday)

"Free from all desires."
But the extinguished candle
Suddenly brings dreams.

Again that ivied castle,
Stillness spiced with wild longing.


The unfinished quest
Resumed, defying fatal
Wisdom, as an ape
Full of appetites defied
Death, gate-crashed Heaven, then left.


Belief in the world—
How subtle this source of fear
Defining Earthlings.
Neither non-existence nor
Existence—fearless foreworld.


Of course, I'm drawn in.
To that extent, an Earthling.
And there are reasons.
Yet I resent the doomers
Who pull on my Earthling strings.


Apocalypse means
No future—choose not the world,
But eternity.
A clip of two friends laughing.
Last Days come and go, like us.

## 8ᵗʰ April (Friday)


The dead outnumber
And the unborn besiege us—
This changeful island.
Bright fusion of scrapbook lives,
Each removed at any time.


To turn to the warmth
That was you and suddenly
It's nowhere—left with
Only the world, everything
Becomes nothing. Sound of trains.


You come to an age
In the changeful Land of Is—
Those you've known longest
Gone soonest. Each unique warmth
Erased, counting down to you.


Red as a coal-fire,
Below the horizon's smoke—
The west-burning sun.

Cold winds, and the clouds so dark
They seem intelligent signs.


The Wild West of tech.
'For your security' means
They're above the law.
They'll track you, spam you, sell you.
Good luck trying to block them.


Someday I'll be forced
To affirm what I believe.
Will I die screaming?
If reality's more than
A scream, then I should say no.


You put the thought off.
Certainty makes itself known.
You will come unglued.
The Great Removal, and no
Vans to take the world with you.


The world's so complex
It makes me nervous. Tonight,
At least, let the moon
Be half a slice of lemon
In a sky too vast to drink.

## 9ᵗʰ April (Saturday)

Picture-book clouds, trees.
Picture-book morning bustle.
Transparent wonder.
Waking as if somewhere strange.
A strangeness that makes me me.


This experience,
Central, extending in all
Directions, mind-spring—
There is this and then there are
Flat, disparate snapshots of me.


The particular,
Like those films the critics hate,
Remains popular.
How the purists fulminate!
Still it involves us daily.


Lo, Jacob's Ladder!
Angels not only ascend,

But also come down.
Mercy on the here and now,
Where first and last are unseen.


### 10th April (Sunday)

Heaven? Hell? Either
Pulls the drawbridge up against
Imagination.
As if we were randomly
Beamed to another planet.


We don't see the end;
It takes us. We grow distant
To ourselves. Our own
Absence buries us. We can't
Come back to give the last word.


What non-sequiturs
Fork the mortal road! To go
From mongrel mundane
To God's nowhere. Even from
Same to same makes my brain squirm.

Where, then, is home? Where
That place we can say "Again"
And mean "Forever"?
Meet again as we should be,
Not forgetting who we were?


### 11<sup>th</sup> April (Monday)

The building rattles.
Below, a phone is answered.
Car radios bleed.
The sound of my own mind or
London's metabolism.


Lying late in bed,
Remembering who I am.
In spite of events,
Which tire, the body resets
Constantly to nought. To me.


Occasional baths
Disappoint me. My elbows
Can't get comfortable.

The water cools too quickly.
My knees—two bony islands.


Explain everything.
Follow the steps they've marked out.
This is how you stay
Engaged. And now there's no time
For that unique source, yourself.


Two kinds of time. Try
Living in subjective time,
At least for a while.
See what follows. Your answers,
To your own questions, not theirs.


### 12<sup>th</sup> April (Tuesday)

I tire of fretting
Over large dooms and little
Sensitivities.
In a universe without
Home, all threats are foregone facts.

We only believe
In science. That's why we have
No medicine for
Our culture—the only true
Realm of possibility.


Literature. Letters.
Tomb-writing. Poetry. Laws.
Records. Accounting.
Text. The net drags us under
And teaches us how to fish.


From this matrix comes,
Perhaps not by accident,
Sometimes poetry:
"Continuously wakened
New horizons." Thus Husserl.


### 13<sup>th</sup> April (Wednesday)

The flat presents new
Symptoms of decrepitude—
A niggling tremor.
Such trivial blights are sent
Just to demoralise me.

Entropy, I s'pose.
The negative of profit—
Life's fatal small print.
Limited energy spent
On plans we can't implement.


Against our very
Weakening we fight, as if
Sighs were our weapons.
With what leaden, dream-like fear
We lose the power to care.


It's harder to do
Anything without the world's
Support. Then again,
Support turns into meddling.
Am I better off ignored?


Sit with me awhile.
Yes, I equivocate but
Hear my presence speak.
Do you sense something hidden?
I'm pregnant with a dragon.

Near the train station,
Apple blossom and the smell
Of fast food outlets.
House of Chicken. Bus stopping.
Shopping, and I'm almost home.


## 14<sup>th</sup> April (Thursday)

I first read this page
Many years ago. It seemed
Dim and grey. Today
I read again, amazed. What
Caused this change? More connections?


The very letters
On the page seem to swell. 'Font'
Reveals its meaning.
What is this fascination?
The textile of connections?


Half intelligence,
At least, is fascination.
Insight drawn by why.

Plato's spark ignites the mind,
Shadowing each word with depth.


But the question's this:
Is that swelling depth made up
Of the massed thickness
Of threads? If so, are single
Threads shallow? Let's look closer.


The path between trees.
I see a tackle of gnats
And know winter's dead.
Close, a wood pigeon murmurs.
This, though lost, is eternal.


### 15<sup>th</sup> April (Friday)

For motivation
I think of converging death
More than of success.
I know I'll die, but success
Seems some delirious tease.

He stuffed the first draft
In a drawer and left it there.
Such needless self-harm.
True! But there were very few
While he lived who stopped and saw.


The translation rut—
From Japanese to English,
It's like robbing graves.
Such shoddy work will never
Draw the readers change requires.


Friend requests. I sigh.
How presumptuous! That is,
Not the presumption
That I'll be friendly, but that
They will be, once they know me.


Perhaps a close-up
On each thread shows finer threads
Again, regressing.
Or else the finest thread in
Very bareness oozes is.

"Filthy habit." Strange
How people repeat certain
Phrases knowingly.
You show what you've picked up, what
Mastered, through simple passwords.


Must be eight o'clock.
Sky pale blue like a bird's egg.
That April full moon.
How much fragrant memory
Humified from such cut grass?


## 16<sup>th</sup> April (Saturday)


The Big Bang, and then
A few sparks and fizzles. Then
Black holes forever.
A flare sent up in dark seas.
We're here, endless night, we're here.


Another planet.
You're stranded and don't even
Know which galaxy.
Awaking there in a cave
You wonder what day it is.

## 17th April (Sunday)

What can it mean: 'Things
Turned out as they were meant to'?
Were they predestined?
Locked in demonstration mode,
A universe shown, not played.


But I think it means
That what has been is enough.
We think of what is
As a mere beginning. Hard
To think of it as finished.

This dandelion's
Sun-dazzled flower, a bee
Probes this way and that.
I think of Schopenhauer.
Something nameless moves all this.

## 18<sup>th</sup> April (Monday)

Every year I send
A card. One year, no reply.
Has someone died? Or
Are they tired of me? Who will
Come to my party this year?


Think of those years, of
Daisy-spangled summer lawns
At Durham. Now think
Of the present, which of all
Possibilities, ensued.


Strange how accurate
That dreadful premonition
Of my childhood was:
I could only be alone.
Poor young heart, who knew me, gone.


But such long life, such
Obscurity—these I feared
Without quite seeing.
Now I see them plainly—here!
For life, too late; death, too soon.

What future chances?
Wounded giants keep fighting.
None will come through whole.
Neglecting souls, we worship
Simulacra of ourselves.


Hybrid? True, but let's
Be less abstract. A thin twig
Grows particular
From thick branches of country,
Era, tongue, creed, family.


Why are city lights
So sad? They don't sigh with us,
Like wind or rain, just
Watch as lives pass by. Hopeless,
Unable to look away.


### 19th April (Tuesday)


"Do you like being
Unhappy?" he asked. At last
I have an answer:

I fear that bright sea—unmoored
On deep waves no foot can tread.


The dark land is firm.
Here we build, sow, harvest crops.
But who is at home
On the sea? And voyages
Take you away for so long.


But the grain I sow
Is bitter. My husbandry
Calls for solitude.
The land I've worked won't outlive
Me, except, at best, as soil.


Rented property—
Never in life to be free
Of wheedling repairs,
Suspense, the borrower's sense
Of shame, fear of homelessness.


What I really need
So my field might yield a world,
Lies over the sea.
Yes, like stories of love. Yes,
And the fishes might shred me.

## 20th April (Wednesday)

Never again to
Enter a railway café,
Slurp some tea and read
A Penguin paperback. From
Small things like these, worlds are made.


For such worlds we fight,
Good protected by evil.
Evil wins both ways.
So that's the future, my friends.
Surrender, fight—evil wins.


Here's a mystery—
That in this blood-smeared vortex,
Good exists at all.
Our model is incomplete.
Confess ignorance; have faith.

## 21ˢᵗ April (Thursday)


I see plainly now
How the world's answers might be
Lying neglected.
The mass of humanity
Don't even see the questions.


The fresh flash of youth—
Unbearable. Another
Volley fired into
The sky of eternity
Misses, falls back to old earth.


Inventive Europe,
In Auden's phrase, which brought us
To this dilemma.
Having come this far, we must
Go farther. How much farther?


Have you thought about
Observational humour?
Just to grasp something
And reproduce it, transforms—
Prehensile fascination.

The first dilemma
Was agriculture, from which
Bands became chiefdoms.
Keeping peace between strangers;
Economy borne by slaves.


Noises of traffic.
The lap-top screen-glow blinks off.
Cinema's message
Is simply this presence, this
Access of world-consciousness.


With cinema we
Dip into world-awareness
As if from outside.
It illustrates deathless mind.
We sense that it's always there.


### 22nd April (Friday)


I missed those phases:
Co-habitation, mortgage,

Marriage, promotion,
Work pension, children, divorce.
The final phase, I won't miss.


I was born a ghost.
No salmon-cycle life-quest,
Dragon and damsel,
No perfect-tense sword: have done.
No. Just birth, ghostliness, death.


Can anxiety
Really be that bad? We seem
To wish above all
To have none of it, even
If the world must be forfeit.


To identify
A thing, do we grasp it twice
And check it against
Itself? Stumped, I can't grasp how
We grasp it in the first place.

## 23rd April (Saturday)

Sometimes now could be
Any time, my mind not yet
Much interfered with.
Then come Time's spies—politics,
Buddhism, situations.


The root of the tongue,
Though silent, allows all speech.
So also, the root
Of the mind, whose beginning,
Slice as you might, you won't find.


Demons with shark-eyes
Sent their final reminder.
But that's blown over.
Making tea, you think: this is
The highest reality.


They learnt how to smile,
First from parents and then friends.
Still my smile is strained.
Quite a simple trick, you'd think,
To make people feel at ease.

## 24<sup>th</sup> April (Sunday)

Those who feel secure—
What do they have in common?
Cuckoos of virtue,
They toss eggs from nests we built,
Lay their do-good brood, then fly.


A demographic,
A whole class, of informers,
Handing you over,
As if they've done the right thing,
Not simply saved their own skins.


They've taken over
The arts. They've taken over
Publishing, the church.
Always laying their pus-filled
Eggs and flying ere they burst.


The large view shows us
The bridge of generations
And no farther shore.
And without the close-up view
Of bolts and girders, it falls.

Neither view tells us
Why we build the bridge, except
Not to fall. The end
We desire and the fall
We shun—both are mysteries.


This holy terror—
That the universe itself
Could be brushed away
Like sand from some greater hand.
We might do well to tremble.


### 25$^{th}$ April (Monday)


Why do I outlive
Mishima, Lovecraft, Dazai?
How young those bygones!
Alone I leave the known roads.
Yes, being born I did so.


So many doubts now,
But once a bureaucracy
Of clerics managed

The awesome formality
Of mortality, for God.


Meaning from my eye
Blisters fascination round
A once-common phrase:
"Temporal goods". Balancing
Books—these and eternal goods.


A heritage since
Decayed like literacy—
The sense that humans
Have something computers don't.
The traitors are still at large.


The insouciance
Of Lord Sebastian Flyte—
Where did all that go?
Nothing left but the shriekers,
Citing Sontag for their hate.


A common error—
People use hyperbole
And then believe it.
The shelves are empty, England
Is dead, the world is ending.

Of course, most people
Are forgotten very soon.
We live forgotten.
Alone in forgetfulness,
I'm the whole world, then I end.

## 26<sup>th</sup> April (Tuesday)

The horrible sense
That empirically, without
Any known reason,
I can't be changed—I'm told this
Paralysis is English.

Though life comes in days,
Somehow the day never comes.
No inventory
Turns life up. Particular?
General? Look and it's not there.

Elusive, precious,
That continuous, unseen
Star, always distant,

Which we keenly fear to lose,
Leads us through scenic nonsense.


The dandelions
In the April soil greet me
With half-noticed smells,
Familiar and dear, yet
For most of life forgotten.


History outstrips
Secondary-world fantasy.
It shows other modes
Of being are possible,
While we lock in to one mode.


The way sticks litter
A footpath, patterning where
Grass becomes patchy
And footfall makes earth bare—what
Palmistry can read such lines?


Approaching the gate,
Woman and boy. She was late
Collecting him, asks,
Was he upset? Promises:
"We'll always come to get you."

The monster's footprints
Are craters of fire. It breathes
And species expire.
I find its trail everywhere.
Spoor still fresh. Will I be next?


Each day infinite—
That parcel, daydream, taste, text.
Zeno was no fool.
How did I traverse all that?
Yet here I am at the end.


### 27ᵗʰ April (Wednesday)


A project in which
You have some small part. You're made
To wait on your own.
The chair is broken. You watch
Motes of dust. Anyway, peace.


Even in such forms,
Mixed with boredom, we must not

Underestimate
How great is the achievement.
Be blessed. There's no shame in it.


Horizons enclose
Worlds. What's beyond, we pretend
To know, or we guess.
The rich have their horizons,
The poor have theirs, little shared.


Only of myself
Can I give. Did Bolan sing
To relieve the poor?
He sang his song; a window
Appeared for hope to peer through.


### 28<sup>th</sup> April (Thursday)


The same sad music.
In every infomercial
The piano plays,
Each tug and swoon of it false,
From YouTube to BBC.

Another letter
About the licence fee. Soon
They will take action.
I've never owned a TV,
But they've threatened me for years.


Yes, sometimes I see
The news at someone's house, or
Hear Radio 4.
"You need us!" they say. But they
Don't want to know who we are.


Interesting. All these
Threats over the licence fee,
And I need you? You!
Who want me guilty, abject,
Voiceless, done for. I need you?


The magic potion
Wears off. Reattuning to
Disenchantment, you
See that all desires can fade—
Even desire for desire.

His life's work was lost.
Decades of carefully filed
Disquisitions, notes,
Spoking an unspoken hub—
A drop of dew from Heaven.


Like an insect caught
In a pond's surface tension,
I'm trapped in fiction.
Everything's material
For a story no one reads.


### 29th April (Friday)


How much solitude
Thinking requires! And reading
And writing claim lives.
Naturally a moat troughs deep
Around the castled scholar.


Strange contradictions
Of the West. "It's NATO's fault."
This very dissent
As if Ukraine were a pawn
To be saved or sacrificed.

Confucius mainly
Lived in wandering exile,
Prized the *Annals* most.
Plato fumbled Syracuse,
Started the longest long march.


The scholar ponders.
Can I, having studied, move
Pieces on the board?
Absurd! And yet I can write
A footnote in the rule book.


The second person
And the first. Separated,
Each knows the other.
The final separation
Makes keen the soul with suspense.


They've known you since birth.
Now they seem like snow, settled
In odd-shaped patches.
Frail, they keep the day's own pace,
Like diaries with blank pages.

It takes interest, time,
Attention to read a book.
Few do. Yet even
Without readers—strange power!—
Somehow a book still offends.


## 30<sup>th</sup> April (Saturday)

What makes my heart beat?
If it weren't automatic,
How would I work it?
Each second, something unknown
Keeps me from non-existence.


Why is the mere nod
Of a head of buddleia
So dear that I don't
Want to leave the world? Am I
Just extending the suspense?


There must be something,
Not indifference, nor clinging,
That will let me go
Having said "Enough", meaning
"I'm full," not "I'm sick of this."

Ravensbourne River.
I'm looking for Bus Stop H.
London's how it was
Again. I'm glad, but can't help
Knowing things are lost each time.


A curved, shady street.
Railings around a garden.
A strange bird questions.
The influence of Venus.
Here, in this place, a portent.

# A PARTIAL LIST OF SNUGGLY BOOKS

**MAY ARMAND BLANC** *The Last Rendezvous*
**G. ALBERT AURIER** *Elsewhere and Other Stories*
**CHARLES BARBARA** *My Lunatic Asylum*
**S. HENRY BERTHOUD** *Misanthropic Tales*
**LÉON BLOY** *The Tarantulas' Parlor and Other Unkind Tales*
**ÉLÉMIR BOURGES** *The Twilight of the Gods*
**ADA BUISSON** *The Baron's Coffin and Other Disquieting Tales*
**CYRIEL BUYSSE** *The Aunts*
**JAMES CHAMPAGNE** *Harlem Smoke*
**FÉLICIEN CHAMPSAUR** *The Latin Orgy*
**BRENDAN CONNELL** *Metrophilias*
**BRENDAN CONNELL (editor)**
  *The Zinzolin Book of Occult Fiction*
**RAFAELA CONTRERAS** *The Turquoise Ring and Other Stories*
**DANIEL CORRICK (editor)**
  *Ghosts and Robbers: An Anthology of German Gothic Fiction*
**ADOLFO COUVE** *When I Think of My Missing Head*
**QUENTIN S. CRISP** *Aiaigasa*
**ALADY DILKE** *The Outcast Spirit and Other Stories*
**ÉDOUARD DUJARDIN** *Hauntings*
**BERIT ELLINGSEN** *Now We Can See the Moon*
**ERCKMANN-CHATRIAN** *A Malediction*
**ALPHONSE ESQUIROS** *The Enchanted Castle*
**ENRIQUE GÓMEZ CARRILLO** *Sentimental Stories*
**DELPHI FABRICE** *Flowers of Ether*
**DELPHI FABRICE** *The Red Spider*
**BENJAMIN GASTINEAU** *The Reign of Satan*
**EDMOND AND JULES DE GONCOURT** *Manette Salomon*
**REMY DE GOURMONT** *From a Faraway Land*
**REMY DE GOURMONT** *Morose Vignettes*
**GUIDO GOZZANO** *Alcina and Other Stories*
**GUSTAVE GUICHES** *The Modesty of Sodom*
**EDWARD HERON-ALLEN** *The Complete Shorter Fiction*
**RHYS HUGHES** *Cloud Farming in Wales*
**J.-K. HUYSMANS** *The Crowds of Lourdes*
**J.-K. HUYSMANS** *Knapsacks*
**COLIN INSOLE** *Valerie and Other Stories*
**JUSTIN ISIS** *Pleasant Tales II*

**JULES JANIN** *The Dead Donkey and the Guillotined Woman*
**GUSTAVE KAHN** *The Mad King*
**MARIE KRYSINSKA** *The Path of Amour*
**BERNARD LAZARE** *The Mirror of Legends*
**BERNARD LAZARE** *The Torch-Bearers*
**MAURICE LEVEL** *The Shadow*
**JEAN LORRAIN** *Errant Vice*
**JEAN LORRAIN** *Fards and Poisons*
**JEAN LORRAIN** *Masks in the Tapestry*
**JEAN LORRAIN** *Monsieur de Bougrelon and Other Stories*
**JEAN LORRAIN** *Nightmares of an Ether-Drinker*
**JEAN LORRAIN** *The Soul-Drinker and Other Decadent Fantasies*
**GEORGES DE LYS** *An Idyll in Sodom*
**GEORGES DE LYS** *Penthesilea*
**ARTHUR MACHEN** *N*
**ARTHUR MACHEN** *Ornaments in Jade*
**CAMILLE MAUCLAIR** *The Frail Soul and Other Stories*
**CATULLE MENDÈS** *Bluebirds*
**CATULLE MENDÈS** *For Reading in the Bath*
**CATULLE MENDÈS** *Mephistophela*
**ÉPHRAÏM MIKHAËL** *Halyartes and Other Poems in Prose*
**LUIS DE MIRANDA** *Who Killed the Poet?*
**OCTAVE MIRBEAU** *The Death of Balzac*
**CHARLES MORICE** *Babels, Balloons and Innocent Eyes*
**GABRIEL MOUREY** *Monada*
**DAMIAN MURPHY** *Daughters of Apostasy*
**KRISTINE ONG MUSLIM** *Butterfly Dream*
**OSSIT** *Ilse*
**CHARLES NODIER** *Outlaws and Sorrows*
**HERSH DOVID NOMBERG** *A Cheerful Soul and Other Stories*
**PHILOTHÉE O'NEDDY** *The Enchanted Ring*
**GEORGES DE PEYREBRUNE** *A Decadent Woman*
**HÉLÈNE PICARD** *Sabbat*
**URSULA PFLUG** *Down From*
**JEAN PRINTEMPS** *Whimsical Tales*
**JEREMY REED** *When a Girl Loves a Girl*
**ADOLPHE RETTÉ** *Misty Thule*
**JEAN RICHEPIN** *The Bull-Man and the Grasshopper*
**DAVID RIX** *A Blast of Hunters*
**FREDERICK ROLFE (Baron Corvo)** *Amico di Sandro*

**JASON ROLFE** *An Archive of Human Nonsense*
**ARNAUD RYKNER** *The Last Train*
**MARCEL SCHWOB** *The Assassins and Other Stories*
**MARCEL SCHWOB** *Double Heart*
**CHRISTIAN HEINRICH SPIESS** *The Dwarf of Westerbourg*
**BRIAN STABLEFORD (editor)**
   *Decadence and Symbolism: A Showcase Anthology*
**BRIAN STABLEFORD (editor)** *The Snuggly Satyricon*
**BRIAN STABLEFORD (editor)** *The Snuggly Satanicon*
**BRIAN STABLEFORD** *Spirits of the Vasty Deep*
**COUNT ERIC STENBOCK** *Love, Sleep & Dreams*
**COUNT ERIC STENBOCK** *Myrtle, Rue & Cypress*
**COUNT ERIC STENBOCK** *The Shadow of Death*
**COUNT ERIC STENBOCK** *Studies of Death*
**MONTAGUE SUMMERS** *The Bride of Christ and Other Fictions*
**MONTAGUE SUMMERS** *Six Ghost Stories*
**ALICE TÉLOT** *The Inn of Tears*
**GILBERT-AUGUSTIN THIERRY**
   *Reincarnation and Redemption*
**DOUGLAS THOMPSON** *The Fallen West*
**TOADHOUSE** *Gone Fishing with Samy Rosenstock*
**TOADHOUSE** *Living and Dying in a Mind Field*
**TOADHOUSE** *What Makes the Wave Break?*
**LÉO TRÉZENIK** *The Confession of a Madman*
**LÉO TRÉZENIK** *Decadent Prose Pieces*
**RUGGERO VASARI** *Raun*
**ILARIE VORONCA** *The Confession of a False Soul*
**JANE DE LA VAUDÈRE** *The Demi-Sexes and The Androgynes*
**JANE DE LA VAUDÈRE**
   *The Double Star and Other Occult Fantasies*
**AUGUSTE VILLIERS DE L'ISLE-ADAM** *Isis*
**RENÉE VIVIEN AND HÉLÈNE DE ZUYLEN DE NYEVELT**
   *Faustina and Other Stories*
**RENÉE VIVIEN** *Lilith's Legacy*
**RENÉE VIVIEN** *A Woman Appeared to Me*
**ILARIE VORONCA** *The Confession of a False Soul*
**ILARIE VORONCA** *The Key to Reality*
**TERESA WILMS MONTT** *In the Stillness of Marble*
**TERESA WILMS MONTT** *Sentimental Doubts*
**KAREL VAN DE WOESTIJNE** *The Dying Peasant*

www.ingramcontent.com/pod-product-compliance
Lightning Source LLC
Chambersburg PA
CBHW020520080526
44583CB00013B/679